Vilém Flusser

NATURAL:MIND

Translated by Rodrigo Maltez Novaes

Flusser Archive Collection

Edited by Siegfried Zielinski

& Norval Baitello Junior

UNIVOCAL

Natural:Mente: vários acessos ao significado de natureza
- published by Duas Cidades, 1979 -

Translated from Portuguese by Rodrigo Maltez Novaes
as *Natural:Mind*

Edited by Siegfried Zielinski and Norval Baitello Junior

First Edition
Minneapolis © 2013, Univocal Publishing

Published by Univocal
123 North 3rd Street, #202
Minneapolis, MN 55401
www.univocalpublishing.com

This book has been published with support from the
Brazilian Ministry of Culture / National Library Foundation.

Obra publicada com o apoio do
Ministério da Cultura do Brasil / Fundação Biblioteca Nacional.

MINISTÉRIO DA CULTURA
Fundação BIBLIOTECA NACIONAL

Published with the support of FAPESP

No part of this book may be reproduced or transmitted in any form
or by any means, electronic or mechanical, including photocopying,
recording or any other information storage or retrieval system,
without prior permission in writing from the publisher.

Thanks to the Vilém Flusser Archive at the Universität der Künste Berlin,
Dinah Flusser, Miguel Flusser, Edith Flusser, Claudia Becker,
Meredith Forbes, Dylan Hester, and Jon Thrower.

Designed & Printed by Jason Wagner
Distributed by the University of Minnesota Press

ISBN 9781937561147
Library of Congress Control Number 2013949336

TABLE OF CONTENTS

Translator's Introduction..IX

Paths..1

Valleys..11

Birds...21

Rain..29

The Cedar in the Park...35

Cows..43

Grass..49

Fingers...57

The Moon..65

Mountains...73

The False Spring..81

Meadows...89

Winds..97

Wonders..105

Buds..113

Fog...121

Natural:Mind..129

Flusser Archive Collection

Vilém Flusser is one of the most influential thinkers of media and cultural theory as well as the philosophy of communication in the second half of the 20th century. But unlike certain thinkers of media culture such as Marshall McLuhan or Jean Baudrillard, most of his work has yet to attain the proper attention of the reading public inside and outside the walls of the academy. One of the reasons for this is due to the singular process by which Flusser constructed his thinking and writing. He is a rare polyglot who would write his texts in various languages until he was satisfied with the outcome. Fluent in Czech, German, French, English, and Portuguese, he has left an archive full of thousands of manuscripts in various languages. The Flusser Archive Collection will be a monumental step forward in finally providing an Anglophone readership with a collection of some of Flusser's most important works.

Translator's Introduction

Vilém Flusser began working on the essays for *Natural:Mind* in 1974, writing the majority during the winter and completing the Portuguese manuscript in March of 1975. Duas Cidades, a publishing house in São Paulo, published *Natural:Mente* in Brazil in 1979, edited by his close friend and correspondent Milton Vargas. In Germany, Hanser published it as *Vogelflüge* in 2000, translated by his wife Edith Flusser. The idea for writing *Natural:Mind* came to him in 1973, one year after the Flussers moved back to Europe after having lived in São Paulo for thirty-two years.

Natural:Mind is the second book of a series in which Flusser started to explore and develop his own style of phenomenological analysis. The first of these titles published in Europe was *La Force du Quotidien* (Editions Mame, 1973), in which Flusser examined "cultural" objects of our daily life such as mirrors, beds, books, etc. The analysis of "natural" objects in *Natural:Mind* is, therefore, a logical progression of this theme. The writing of *Gesten*, a phenomenological study of human gestures, quickly followed in 1976 and was initially published in German by Bollmann Editions in 1991, the year that Flusser died. In 1979, Flusser wrote the last title of the series, *Pós-História*, published by Duas Cidades in 1983.

In some of his letters exchanged with Vargas, Flusser tried to clarify what his intentions were and how he engaged methodologically with the subject. In the course of gradually sending the essays to Vargas in small groups, he added a short comment in a letter dated February 5, 1975:

> After you have read the texts, you shall verify the aim: to analyze objects taken to be "natural" by common sense, in order to illuminate, from as many points of view as possible, the problematic of such a classifying label. The collection of proposed essays really seeks to be "essayistic": rough and experimental. (Essay is a literary form between poetry, philosophy, pamphlet, and journalism, therefore: "post" all of these.) My masters, as you shall verify, are Bachelard and Ortega [y Gasset]. However I take a different path. I seek "to inventory," that is: to open a field for a future disciplined study. In these essays, I am more within the field of a "formalist" tradition and less within the tradition of an existential phenomenology (although strongly nourished by it). And, although less polemic than Bachelard and Ortega, I am, I believe, more engaged. In sum: I am of a different generation.

One month later, in another letter to Vargas dated March 8, 1975, Flusser adds:

"Nature": Agreed: once I have finished the essays I will write the introduction [...] But my dear friend: it is not just a case of seeing only two alternatives for the interpretation of the term "nature." You mention "physis" (which I described in "The False Spring"), and the "aorgic" (which I have not described yet). [...] And here are a few other: nature-creation, nature-object, nature-raw material, nature-stage, nature-condition, nature-freedom, nature-sin, nature-salvation, nature-exuberance, and nature-journey. And finally, let's consider what the "bishop"[1] says in Faust: Natur und Geist: so spricht man nicht zu Christen. Dafuer verbrennt man Atheisten, Weil sie gar boes und gar des Teufels sind. Natur ist Hoelle, Geist ist Teufel, Sie hegen zwischen sich den Zweifel, Ihr missgestaltet Zwitterkind.[2] (Nature and spirit: do not speak of this to Christians. That is why atheists are burned. These are evil and diabolic things. Nature is hell, and spirit the Devil. Between them they beget doubt, their malformed bastard child.)[3] Of course: Goethe is an atheist and sold his soul to Mephisto. But his "bishop" must be taken seriously nonetheless. In the introduction I will seek to also point out the dialectic "nature-mind" as the Devil's trap.

---

1 These lines, from Goethe's *Faust part II*, are in fact spoken by the chancellor. But when writing letters, Flusser rarely checked his sources, therefore his citations are always slightly off.

2 The correct text is: Natur und Geist—so spricht man nicht zu Christen. Deshalb verbrennt man Atheisten, Weil solche Reden hoechst gefaehrlich sind. Natur ist Suende, Geist ist Teufel, Sie hegen zwischen sich den Zweifel, Ihr missgestaltet Zwitterkind.

3 This is a translation of Flusser's own rendering in Portuguese.

The style of the text in the four books of this series marks a gradual departure for Flusser. During the 1960s, when he first started to publish his work in Brazil, he was lecturing regularly at the Brazilian Institute of Philosophy and at the Polytechnic School of the University of São Paulo, as well as writing for the *O Estado de São Paulo* newspaper. At the time, these activities were strong influences on his writing style: his essays written for lectures were of a condensed but fluid style, to be read out loud to students, but his books of the same period have a more formal style and structure. Toward the end of the 1960s, his style started to become more unified and fluid, and the first half of the 1970s became a period of stylistic experimentation when he returned to Europe. During this period, he wrote to Vargas in a letter dated February 20, 1973:

> Subjective report: I don't know how to write in French, therefore I have been writing in English and Portuguese. But the new experiences penetrate nonetheless through every pore. I have rediscovered Husserl (and, characteristically therefore, Kant on one side and Ortega y Gasset on the other) in my belly. […] My rediscovery of Husserl is reflected in As Coisas que Me Cercam [La Force du Quotidien] (for example in [the essay] "books," which I sent to you. Kant, of whom I wrote to you from Megève, is reflected in my methodology, especially the Kant of the [Critique of] Practical Reason. And Ortega is once again my stylistic and aesthetic master. (Especially of "On Hunting.") On revient toujours a son première amour (Sic).

When Flusser started to engage with the essays for *Natural:Mind*, his style was already close to what it would eventually become in the late 1970s and 1980s: fluid and informal. For example, the frequent use of words in parenthesis with inverted commas as in: ("example"), is a particular visual element that he experimented with in some of his essays. Although some of these visual elements gradually disappear in later texts, they endow *Natural:Mind* with a very particular "feeling" within Flusser's oeuvre. He also experimented with the structure of the essays, allowing each to follow a path dictated by the particular phenomenon being analyzed rather than conforming to a strict formal analysis and notation of the subject at hand. This approach is more poetic than scientific. As he allows himself to enter into an internal conversation with a specific phenomenon it becomes reflected in the structure of the text, which becomes guided by the "voice" given to the phenomenon he has chosen to engage with. In other words, *Natural:Mind* is a window into this internal dialogue, through which Flusser allows us to peek into his thought process, rather than presenting us the "facts" he collected in the "field."

Flusser intended to publish the book first in France in 1974, following the publication of *La Force du Quotidien*. Unfortunately, this did not happen and as a result Flusser dropped the project for some time, but when he took up the project once again at the end of 1974, encouraged by Vargas, Flusser was still referring to the project by its initial working title in French, which was *Ça Existe la Nature?* (*Does Nature Exist?*). However, Flusser expressed his doubts about it in his letters to Vargas, as he felt that it was a rather literal title. When he finished writing the final essays in March of 1975, Flusser chose the adverb *naturalmente* (naturally) as the title for the Portuguese version of the book, which he communicated to Vargas on the note that accompanied the last set of essays on March 17, 1975. The addition of a colon in the final Portuguese title was a last minute flash of inspiration just as the book was about to go to press. The graphic separation of the root and the suffix, *natural:mente*, created a phrase out of the same word and thus added a second layer of meaning that transformed the title into a concrete poem. When writing in English, Flusser refers to the book as "*Natural:Mind*" so I have kept the title in the same form. In English the double layer of meaning is obviously lost, therefore *Natural:Mind* – a mind that is naturally minded.

Rodrigo Maltez Novaes
Berlin, 2013

Natural:Mind

PATHS
(a kind of introduction)

Two experiences are converging in order to form the whirlpool of reflections to be reported here. The first is the last time that the author crossed the Fuorn Pass, which joins the Engadin Valley to the range of valleys of the Trentino-Alto Adige on the borders with Italy, Austria and Switzerland. The second is the author's recent visit to the stones of Carnac in Brittany. But before allowing for these experiences to converge, the author must first describe them.

The Fuorn Pass is an asphalt road, it is not very wide because it does not have a heavy flow of traffic as it connects regions that are not so densely populated. However, it is kept clear of snow throughout all of winter, when other more important roads are closed to traffic because there is no alternative connection between the regions that it joins. The Fuorn Pass is a subsidiary road of the great artery that starts at Chur and goes toward Milan through the Maloja Pass, which forms one of the central European north-south passages. It leaves from an artery at Zernez, in the Engadin Valley (not very far from St. Moritz, the city of American millionaires and oil sheiks, and of Sils Maria, that of the Zarathustrian

Nietzsche), goes up through the Engadin National Park up to a height of two thousand three hundred meters, goes down through the Vinschgau Valley with its Ladin villages and its Gothic and Lombardic castles. It continues through the Trentino-Alto Adige Valley, where it becomes entwined with the road that Drusus built in order to defeat the Rhaetians, and reaches at Bolzano (the classic "*Pons Drusi*") the Munich-Rome motorway, which is, in its turn, the Via Flaminia, through which Germanicus penetrated the Teutonic forests in the name of Rome. And through which, in the opposite direction, the emperor Henry IV travelled penitently in order to surrender, at Canossa, the crown of the Holy Roman Empire to the authority of the Roman Pope. So by transversally connecting two major arteries, the Fuorn Pass road (a Ladin name, which obviously means the Oven Pass) seems to be a work of recent engineering, aimed at relieving some of the heavy traffic of trucks that run, as an uninterrupted chain, between central Europe and the Italian peninsula: a recent and daring work of engineering that demanded the application of the most advanced technological methods.

The author travelled through it several times, and always admired not only the majestic view of the peaks and glaciers, but also the beauty of its curves. There, the human spirit, armed with the instruments of science, managed to literally bore through the secrets of nature and open them up to contemplation, and it managed to do so in the form of beauty. Or so the author believed, until he read in a book on paleoanthropology that the Fuorn Pass was, for countless millennia, the path for herds of horses, "Ur" cattle, and reindeer, a path which they crossed while being chased by Paleolithic hunters, our ancestors. The route of today's road was "built" by those herds. The project of the road belongs to the horses, cattle, and reindeer. It is only the contemporary execution which is a product of human labor, as countless previous versions must have been. If project and idea are considered as related concepts, then the idea to create the road was had by the animals of the tundra. They were the ones who dared. And we, who travel by car from Bolzano to Zernez, are only following their footsteps, exactly as our ancestors, the hunters, did.

Whoever travels to Brittany, as the author did last week, penetrates a mysterious region, for a multitude of reasons: because of the curious constructions called "calvaries," which characterize it; because of Mont Saint-Michel, that monastic monster, that Mount Athos of the West; because of the pseudo-Christian legends of the Bretons that moved there after having been expelled from "great" Britain by the Anglo-Saxons, and who continue to "Bretonize" there to this day, even though their language and culture have disappeared from the English homeland a long time ago; because of that very curious Celtic people called "the people of the sea = Armoricaine," which was never really dominated by the Romans, not even by the Gauls, the Bretons, or the Franks, and, by the way, not even by the Parisian bourgeoisie who are building their apartment blocks on the "Armoricaine" beaches. (But they are being dominated, along with the rest of the West, by mass culture, so that they are currently going from being "Armoricaine" to becoming Americans.) However, the region is mysterious especially because of the peoples that anteceded the Armoricaines, about whom very little is known, except that they built (if "build" is the right term), between six and four thousand years before Christ, those sets of wonderful stones at Carnac and on the other side of the channel at Stonehenge. Who were those people, who, more than two thousand years before the first Egyptian pyramid was built, were absurdly raising thousands of pointed and irregular stones, hundreds of which weigh several times the weight of the obelisk at the Place de la Concorde, whose erection demanded the maximum effort of the Enlightenment's technical abilities, and all of the romantically revolutionary ardor of the French Republic? The author has not found, until now, in the books that he consulted, a satisfactory answer to this question. He has found only fantastic interpretations of the "dawn of the magicians" sort, or banal interpretations of the Freudian "phallus." These interpretations and others that are similar are unsatisfactory, because when faced with every human work, there emerges the question as to the motive or purpose of such work. This is what distinguishes culture from nature: cultural works have meaning, they are decodable. The rocks of Carnac are absurdly mysterious, because we have lost the key to the code that endows them with meaning. We no longer know why or for what purpose they were erected, and we are obliged to "interpret them" instead of being able to "read them."

The thousands of rocks that cover the plains around the village of fishermen and "Belonnes" oyster famers, called Carnac (a name mysteriously suggestive of Egypt, which also points to a past beyond the Bronze Age because of its suffix "-ac"), seem, at first sight, to be a collection of chaotically spread ruins, as if a building of transhuman proportions had collapsed during an earthquake. However, the observer slowly discovers that what seems to be chaos is in fact an ultra-complex order. The rocks do not seem, under more careful observation, to be types of statues like "*objects trouvés*" or "minimal art" of gigantic proportions, but elements of invisible or vanished fences. And these super-fences, when mentally reconstructed, start to delineate hundreds of paths that crisscross within a highly sophisticated geometric design. Through the mind's eye there emerges a collection of colossal avenues and streets within which the individual rocks become only an element of delineation, despite their gigantic proportions. And if the rocks themselves are transformed into dwarfs within such a labyrinth, what then, becomes of us humans? We become ants that run, disorientated, within these avenues and streets that were built for beings of a different scale, who seek to touch, with our mental antennae, the individual rocks in order to discover the beings that walked these avenues in other times. Without a doubt: the rocks were put in their particular places by people like us, but with efforts and methods that are difficult to imagine. Yet the project of construction could not very well have originated from these people's minds. The construction cannot have served any of their needs. Such a project must have had a different origin, and must have been "inspired" in some way within the minds of those who built it. As they constructed the "alignments" of Carnac, those people who we ignore, the inhabitants of a pre-Egyptian Brittany, must have obeyed projects that they were unaware of, with the aim of opening paths for purposes of which they were also unaware.

Both experiences reported here converge upon the same point: the project of paths. And the reflections gyrate rapidly on this point in centrifugal circles, since "project" and "paths" are terms loaded with meaning. Such a fugue from the center may, however, be disciplined, if thought grasps a single (let us say "concrete") aspect of the problem that presents itself when the two experiences converge. This: the projects of human paths are not necessarily human. In the case of the Fuorn Pass, the project seems to have been pre-human, and in the case of the alignment of the rocks of Carnac, it seems to have been extra-human. If thought grasps this aspect, it then becomes possible for the distinction between two types of paths: the ones projected, traced, imagined and programmed by clear, distinct and conscious deliberation; and the other ones. Examples of the first type would be the Monumental Axis of Brasilia and the Transamazonian motorway, and examples of the second would be the Fuorn Pass and Carnac. This distinction may contribute to a deepening of the dialectic comprehension of nature.

We are tempted to affirm that the difference between consciously deliberated paths and the others arises from their age. The old paths, the pre-historic ones, would be those whose plans and projects fell into oblivion, and because of that, they seem to us late observers not to have been deliberated upon. The phenomena do not, however, confirm such an affirmation. The salt and amber paths that cross Europe are very old, but reveal, all the same, deliberate projects. And the Fuorn Pass is one of the most recent alpine paths. The affirmation that the older the path is, the less artificial, and therefore the more "natural" it is, cannot be sustained. The natural or artificial nature of a path is not a function of its age. It cannot be, since history is not simply a process of ever-increasing artificialization, but a process that returns periodically to the natural sources from which it springs. Another attempt to explain the difference must be explored.

Maybe this: the four examples of paths suggested in this essay may be regrouped, having as criterion not their project, but the function they serve. The Fuorn Pass and the Transamazonian motorway serve to transport goods and people; Carnac and the Monumental Axis of Brasilia serve as symbols, they transport messages. Clearly, the criterion is exclusivist. The Monumental Axis is also a channel through which functionaries of several Ministries drive to work, and the roads of Carnac must have also served as roads for "druids." And the Fuorn Pass and the Transamazonian motorway are also symbols of something (the first, maybe of a Common Market, the second, certainly of a Greater Brazil). However, the symbolic function predominates in one of the pairs, and the economic function in the other; thus, if we depart from the criterion of function, the difference between deliberately projected paths and the others becomes clearer.

The Fuorn Pass is a far more technically elaborate road than the Transamazonian motorway, which is nothing more than dirt-road for large stretches. In this sense, the Fuorn Pass is more "artificial," more "culture" and less "nature." However, the Transamazonian imposes itself a lot more upon the landscape that it crosses; it advances not only through it but also against it. It devours the forest, while the Fuorn Pass highlights the landscape. In this sense the Transamazonian is a lot more artificial and cultural: it represents, even more so, the victory of human deliberation over the natural conditions imposed on humans. The code to which the Monumental Axis belongs as symbol (an airplane that takes off into a bright future, the dawn, Big Brazil, etc.) is a lot more denotative, clear, and distinct than the code to which Carnac belongs, and not only because we have lost the key. Carnac's code must have always been obscure and highly connotative. The message from the Monumental Axis demands, therefore, a different reading from that of Carnac: more intellectual than intuitive. In this sense the Monumental Axis is much more artificial and cultural than Carnac: it represents, much more clearly, the human will to give meaning to the world, so that the artificiality of a path seems to not depend on its elaboration, or even on its function, but rather on the existential climate that surrounds it. Through "artificial" and "cultural" paths, humanity walks upright toward a destiny that they themselves projected. Through mysterious and "natural" paths, humanity follows the steps of ignored or vaguely intuited beings, into an ignored or vaguely intuited future. Or, as in Carnac, without an apparent aim. And since there are these two types of paths, there are also two types of "*Homo viator.*"

However, such a distinction between "natural" and "artificial" paths suggests, at first sight, entirely unsatisfactory concepts of "art" and "culture." "Culture," according to such a criterion, would be the deliberate imposition of a human meaning upon the meaningless set of elements that is "nature," and "art" would be the method through which the human spirit imposes itself upon nature. Although many may effectively espouse such a concept, it is entirely unsatisfactory, and the contemplation of the Fuorn Pass and Carnac prove it. If it were satisfactory, the Transamazonian would be seen as cultural progress over the Fuorn Pass, and the Monumental Axis would be a more meaningful work of art than Carnac, because in the Transamazonian and the Monumental Axis the human spirit imposes itself more clearly upon the nature of the plains and the forest. In reality, the Fuorn Pass presents itself as a work of art as it allows for powerful experiences (by revealing "visions of reality"), and Carnac presents itself as testament of a lost and forgotten culture, but is just as significant and "valid" as ours. Therefore, anti-natural paths are not necessarily fruits of a more "evolved" art, and culture is not necessarily anti-nature.

Both types of paths, suggest, on the contrary, that there are two types of culture, each of which applies art differently. The first type of culture would be the product of the effort to always elaborate and make the essence of nature more resplendent, and its art would be the method through which such essence is revealed. The Fuorn Pass and Carnac would be works of this type of culture. The second type of culture would, effectively, be the product of the deliberate effort to always impose human projects upon nature and to make the essence of the human spirit more resplendent, and its art would be the method through which such essence is revealed. The Transamazonian and the Monumental Axis would be works of this type of culture. However, such schematization simplifies the problem. The two types of art and culture probably do not exist, and have never existed in a pure state. Every concrete culture and every art are, probably, a mixture or synthesis of the two proposed types. This makes it extremely problematic, not only to want to distinguish, ontologically, between several cultures, but also to want to establish a rigorous dialectic between culture and nature.

This implies that *Homo viator* is not a being who can choose between deliberate and mysterious paths, or who can do it deliberately or spontaneously. It implies, on the contrary, that *Homo viator* is a being who walks sometimes on deliberate paths, sometimes on mysterious paths, and that he does it sometimes deliberately, sometimes spontaneously; and that, in the majority of cases, he walks partially deliberately and partially spontaneously, on partially deliberate and partially spontaneous paths. Because with the Fuorn Pass and Carnac on one side, and the Transamazonian motorway and the Monumental Axis of Brasilia on the other, these are in fact borderline cases ("*Grenzsituationen*"). The majority of the paths are like the Autostrada del Sole or the Via Dutra, or as the Rue de Seine or the Rua Direita, more or less poorly planned, and that are "poorly" planned because there the human spirit did not manage to impose itself completely. It is through these paths that we walk, as a general rule.

VALLEYS

We have several ways of relating to nature, some of which may be called "supernatural," "theoretical," or "perspectival" (according to our many tastes). One of these ways is to see nature as a map. In this view, we have inverted the epistemological relation between landscape and map. The map no longer represents the landscape, but now it is the landscape that represents the map. The map no longer serves as an instrument so that we may orient ourselves in the landscape, but now it is the landscape that serves as an instrument so that we may orient ourselves in the map. The truth stops being a function of the map's adjustment to the landscape, and becomes a function of the landscape's adjustment to the map. Such a furious idealism, drummed into our heads during high school, expresses itself in the sentence "the sea is blue, and the English dominions are red." Under this view, valleys become the paths through which the water runs toward the ocean. Is this the "scientific" view?

We have, in this case, a particular model: that of water circulation. Here, the origin of the model does not matter. The model foresees (in the sense of "telling" or "prophesizing") that one of the phases of the water cycle is the running of the water down the mountains through the valleys. The observation of the landscape confirms the model. Or in other words: the landscape adapts itself to the model (the "map"). It answered "yes." Valleys are affirmative answers to the "spiritual" investigation (formal) of the map. Madness? Yes, in the sense of "spirit" as madness, of man as a mad animal. And not in the sense of "spirit" as negation, of man as an animal that can change valleys by building dams. For an engineer, this vision of the valley is "adequate." For those who live in the valley, it is madness. But is it possible that engineers cannot live in valleys? They cannot. As engineers, they live in the maps.

I am not an engineer and I live in a valley. Or do I? Even though I am not an engineer, I am also man: a mad animal. I, too, was expelled from paradise, not just the engineers. I cannot live in the valley, or at least, not completely. I also live, partially, in the realm of engines, even though my engines are not the ones of the engineer. I do not practice "natural science," as the engineer does. I am, poor me, a humanist. My madness is of another kind. Valleys for me are also paths. Certainly not for water, but paths for men. Here is why I cannot live so completely in the valley as the deer do. Deer roam in the valley and I walk through it. I cross the valley (be it the valley of tears or of smiles). *Homo viator*. Errant knight, errant Jew. Stranger. But not completely. If I walk through the valley of the shadow of death, you are with me. How green therefore is my valley! However, the valley is mine, and I am not its, because I also have a map, to which my valley must answer "yes or no" to adjust itself. My map, my engine, is this:

Humanity is a horde of invaders, of immigrants. It has invaded the landscape for approximately eight million years, in several waves: searching for reindeer, mammoths, grasses, cattle, salt, coal, and electricity; in sum, in search of happiness. Where the horde comes from is unknown. This is probably a false question; there is no method to answer it. However, it does not seem to be "false," since eight million years is not such a long time after all. But where the horde goes is known. It climbs. It climbs along the rivers and streams in the opposite direction that the water runs. It climbs the valleys. The valleys are the arteries through which the blood of humanity's river climbs. And the narrow mountain valleys are the capillaries. In them the invasion stagnates. They are dams, in the opposite sense from that of the engineer's. In my map, the first are the last: the most courageous standard bearers, who form the tip of the invading spear, and who penetrate the narrowest valleys, remain dammed there in order to form the last vestiges of the horde. I live (in the problematic sense of the term) in a narrow mountain valley. Now my valley, answer me, "yes or no?" Answer my "perspectivist," historicist, humanist question.

During the last interglacial period, this valley was probably inhabited by men of the Heidelberg species, when at the same time the lower plains were inhabited by *Homines sapientes*. When the plains were already Neolithic and grass was planted, here the Alpine goats were still Paleolithically hunted. When Rhaetian was being spoken in the plains and bronze was already used, here there were still Neolithic villages without division of labor. Here, Rhaetian was spoken when Latin and

Greek were already spoken in the plains (and elsewhere). When middle German dominated the Holy Empire, here Ladin was spoken. Today German is spoken here, when it is Italian that is spoken in the plains. Yet in the small side valleys Ladin is still spoken. And Rhaetian still has not died in small agglomerations above three thousand meters. And there are still houses built in the Neolithic way. And there are small isolated ponds at the foot of the glaciers, where people still fish in the Paleolithic way. And are there not Neanderthal and Heidelberguian traces on the faces of the mountain people? My valley has answered: "yes, I am structured according to your map." I live in a dam of human history, in which "anterior" becomes "the higher valley," and "posterior" the "lower valley." This type of stratification is contrary to that of geology. Unsurprisingly: the "humanities" have a different map than that of the "natural sciences." Time runs in opposite directions according to both disciplines. In the natural sciences, it runs toward entropy; in the humanities, toward increasing information. The water runs in the opposite direction from that of the river of humanity. The historical stratification of my valley is in opposition to its geological stratification, just like the "spirit" is in opposition to the world, because the world is a passage, and "spirit" is adventure.

My valley is not interesting only for the fact that I live in it. It may be generalized. Is this not how the "spirit" functions: generalizing, classifying, and projecting "high?" That is: emptying? My concrete valley could here be generalized into an empty form: "a class of valleys." That is why it is interesting. It may serve as a concrete example of the abstract class "valleys," therefore, as an epistemological inversion. My valley is interesting because once this inversion is done, it allows for this type of question: tradition or progress? On my map, valleys are the places toward which progress advances and where it stagnates. But there, it stagnates in a particular structure: as the structure of "memory," in the Platonic, biological, psychological and cybernetic sense (and maybe also in other senses). On my map, valleys are storage for information, they are conserves, therefore, traditional conservatives. On my map, progress runs uphill in order to be stored in the narrow valleys. On my map, the aim of progress is to be conserved. This is because my map is a humanist's map, not an engineer's. That is why the valley's "*nunc stans*" appears to be an aim of the "*panta rhei,*" or in sum, as Shangri-La. All of humanism is utopian: it aims at the narrow plenitude of the valley, and sees in the wide vacuity of the plains as only one stage of the course.

First attempt at an answer: valleys are articulated. They are narrow and surrounded by obstacles that allow only a few difficult passages. This articulation turns them "organic," that is, difficult to mechanize. They cannot be easily filled with "masses" that move mechanically. It is not possible to easily build in them pharaonic pyramids, *circuses maxima*, or fifty-story banks. Such things do not fit well in valleys, and not because they are "small." The experience of the valley is grandiose, the mountains that surround them are much higher than the tallest pyramids, circuses, and banks. They are not good for "mass" culture, not because valleys are "small," but because they are articulated. The massifying progress of the plains is, therefore, destined to become articulated ("humanized") in the valleys.

Second attempt at an answer: valleys shelter. Every valley forms a universe, with its own fauna and flora, slightly different from that of the next valley, with its own economy, social structure, architecture, music, and legends. And these universes that are the valleys do not communicate with each other, except with the plains, which are common to all. It is in this sense that valleys shelter: not in the sense of isolation from the rest of the world, but in the sense of indirect communication via large roundabouts. This is perhaps what distinguishes the cultures that spring from a network of narrow valleys, from the cultures of the plains: they are "confederative," not "federal," as are the ones from the plains. For example: Greek, Jewish, Tibetan, Toltec and Incan cultures compared to Roman, Mesopotamian, Hindu, Mayan and Chibchan cultures. The "civilizations" of the plains are therefore destined to become cultured in the valleys.

Other similar answers are possible and easy to formulate. All of them will say that history is a process that has the valley as an aim. Or that a happening is a process that has memory as an aim. Or that progress is a process that has tradition as an aim. In sum, they will all say that to store information (negentropy) is humanity's aim. And they will all say that valleys (memories, tradition, negentropy) are not static places, where nothing ever happens. They are, on the contrary, places where information is constantly regrouped and restructured. To speak communicologically: valleys are places where discourses from the plains are dialogued.

That is why valleys are the places for thinkers and poets, from Heraclitus to Nietzsche, David to Rilke. But not for prophets. Prophets do not inhabit valleys. My map does not encompass prophets. I must widen it.

Prophets pass through the valleys and climb all the way to the mountain's summit. They go one step beyond the valley's inhabitants, and then they return. On the way back they do not even rest in the valley that they cross. They go directly to the plains in order to tell their "news." They tell of the view they had on the summit. For them, the valley is a channel between the plain and the summit, and the summit and the plain: an ambivalent channel. On the way up, it is a channel between redundancy and noise. On the way back, it is a channel between noise and new information. On the way up, it is a channel between mass alienation and solitude. On the way back, it is a channel between solitude and engagement. Here is what the valley is, in a map projected from the mountain's summit: no longer a dam, but the place in between. In this map, whoever is in the valley is in the middle of their life. And the question that emerges in such a map is this: is the one who is in the valley still climbing or already going down? Is he still a thinker (the re-formulator of the plain's discourse, of "prose"), or is he already a poet (the preparer of a new discourse)?

Therefore, in this second map (which is no longer historicist, but just as formal as the engineer's map), humanity no longer appears in the form of a river over the valleys, but in the form of a circulation that gyrates in the opposite direction to that of the water. They go up through the capillaries of narrow valleys, some drops project all the way up to the summits and then return laden with "news" in order to vivify the plains. This circulation of humanity climbs up as great rivers (the great "tendencies"), ramifies into deltas at the mountains (the several "heresies"), reaches the summits as individual drops (the great "heretics"), which then evaporate and re-condense into vivifying rain ("prophecy"). Consequently, in this second map, valleys are different paths than the ones in the first map. They are no longer paths that lead toward an aim. They are initiation paths for a return. "Decisive" paths.

He who has never climbed through a valley has never lived. He vegetates in the plains. For him, the third-dimension, that of the sublime, is missing. But he who has climbed through the valley and stayed there also did not live. It is true that he uprooted and de-alienated himself, but he remained hovering in the air, in availability. He must decide to climb higher, to isolate himself ever further on those summits that Rilke called "those of the heart," those that not even eagles inhabit, and to risk himself in the solitude in which Unamuno says he "lost his truth." But in such a decision he cannot wait for a Virgil, or a Godot, or any alpine guide. Or, he must decide to go back to the plains, without having had the risk of the climb, certainly not to be re-integrated, but to engage, because integration has become impossible for those who were in the valley, because for him, integration has now become a synonym of promiscuity. For having climbed the valley he is apocalyptic, and will never go back to being integrated. The "return" can never cancel the "going." Whoever comes back is no longer the same; he is altered. He is informed even if he did not climb to the summit. Here is the decision that whoever has climbed through the valley must make: solitude without the guarantee of a return, or a return without having seen the summit.

Those who were born in the valleys do not see the summits. They look at the soil they cultivate, and rarely at the plains at their feet, where they exchange the products of their labor. They rarely look at the plains, because it is generally covered in mist. That is why those who were born in the valleys believe that they were born above the clouds. They are mistaken. They were born in the middle of the path. Those who were born in the plains and have never left are likewise mistaken. They believe that they were born under the sky, when in reality they were born under the mist that does not allow them to see the valleys or the summits. But those who were born in the plains and climbed up through the valleys see the steep and inaccessible summits first. Then they see the bright green grass of the valley. However, as they are travellers, they see the landscape as if it were a confirmation of the maps they carry in their pockets. Two maps: the first shows the valley as a path that leads to an objective; the second shows the valley as an epicycle that leads to a return. The first map was projected in the heavy climate of the plains and seeks to free the traveller. The second map was projected in the valley itself, and seeks to change the plains and their climate. Both maps are equally adequate. The landscape, if consulted, answers "yes" to both. The decision: "which of the two maps should I use?" cannot be made having the maps as a basis, not even on the basis of a comparison between the maps, on the basis of a "meta-map." It would not be more appropriate for being "meta." Both are equally appropriate. The decision to be made must be "absurd" (without basis).

And this represents the limit of the madness that is the human spirit. It is perfectly possible to project maps. It is perfectly possible to invert the relation between map and landscape, and to consult, not the map in order to orient oneself in the landscape, but the landscape in order to orient oneself in the map. Such madness is perfectly possible. But in terms of making decisions, maps are no good. Authentic decisions are absurd. And the absurd is the concrete (the unclassifiable, non-generalizable, non-formalizable). Once the decision is made, the madness disappears. The decision occurs in the concrete. Valleys are the paths of decisions, concrete places in which it becomes necessary, at a given moment, to throw away all the maps, under the pain of hovering in the "supernatural," the "theoretical," and the "perspectival." Precisely because valleys are almost supernatural, almost theoretical, almost perspectival, they are borderline situations. The decision in them, according to Jaspers, is of deciphering and not of resolving. In sum, valleys are places where availability can, if so decided, become engagement.

Birds

We cannot experience their flight as our ancestors did: as an impossible desire. Birds are no longer those beings that inhabit the space between the sky and us, they have now transformed into beings that occupy the space between our cars and our passenger airplanes. From being the link between animal and angel they have become objects for the study of group behavior. If we want to frame our experience of birds within that of our ancestors', then we should say that for us all birds are what chickens were for them: beings that fly, but that do so precariously. Thus, such a modification of our attitude in relation to birds and to flight (provoked by aviation and astronautics) has a significant effect on our view of the world. We have lost one of the dimensions of the traditional ideal of "freedom," and we have lost the concrete aspect of the traditional vision of the "sublime."

The attempt to intuit the vision that our ancestors had of flight is made difficult by two factors: by our own vision of flight and by the myth of flight. Both of these difficulties break our link with tradition in two opposite ways: the first excludes us from the tradition and the second makes us participate in it in a completely new way. In other words: because we have a different view of the flight of birds, we cannot adequately comprehend how our elders saw them. And because we participate in the same myth of flight, we cannot comprehend how our elders adjusted their view of flight to the myth. I shall try to illustrate both difficulties.

Let us observe three types of bird flight: the hawk, the humming-bird, and the swallow. Three models are spontaneously offered in order to grasp them: the hawk flies like a glider, the humming-bird like a helicopter, and the swallow like a fighter jet. If we try to reflect on the three models, we will verify that their relation to the phenomena they emulate is complex: the three apparatus of modular flight are partial copies of those birds and are partially the result of a development that only became viable after the birds were abandoned as models for flight. Therefore, to take flying apparatus as models of birds is not the classic inversion "modeled – model" that characterizes the majority of our perspectives of things. We comprehend arms as levers because arms were the models for levers, and we see mirrors as the surfaces of lakes because the surfaces of lakes were the models for mirrors. However, we see birds as flying apparatus, even though such apparatus did not have birds but aerodynamic equations as models. In this sense, airplanes are less "natural" instruments than levers and mirrors: they do not have natural things as models. And if we emulate the flight of birds with aviation models (and we do it spontaneously), then we are spontaneously de-naturalizing such a flight.

Our ancestors must have had other models in order to grasp the three types of models. The hawk must have flown like a cloud, the humming-bird as musical notes, and the swallow as an arrow. (Other models are also suggested by literature, our source of comprehension of our elders' vision of the world.) But for us, such a traditional vision of flight is necessarily poeticized and kitsch; that is, sentimentally false. Whoever says today that humming birds float like musical notes (and not that they hover in vertical flight above flowers), is being insincere because the model of the helicopter imposes itself spontaneously. To wish to see the flight of birds as our ancestors did is to wish to turn such flight into something kitsch, and this illustrates the first difficulty.

The myth of flight, as it is manifested in countless mythologies and countless dreams, and as it inspired countless dreamers, from the tailor of Ulm and Leonardo da Vinci to Jules Verne and NASA, continues to be active within us just as it was for our elders. Incidentally, the thesis according to which myths are constant "projects" that provoke history but that cannot be overcome by history seems to be deeply rooted in psychology as well as in sociology. However, the same myth has an entirely different impact on those who have the experience of flight than it had on our ancestors, for whom to fly was an impossible dream. If we fly by jet-plane from São Paulo to Paris we are overtaken by an ambivalent sensation: on the one hand we know that we flew "better" than hawks (higher, farther, and faster), and that therefore our reality is overcoming our myth. But on the other hand we feel that to fly in jet-planes is not the "message" of the myth and that it could not have been what inspired Icarus and Leonardo da Vinci. As it was no longer an impossible dream, the myth became an undreamable dream, however, it persists. If one of the basic theses of Marxism is that dreams are killed once they are realized, then the dialectic side of such a thesis is forgotten: dead dreams persist. Of course, we can fly, and we can do it "better" than Leonardo dreamed, but we simultaneously prefer Leonardo's dream to our reality. And it is no use if we call the Fiumicino Airport (this characteristic vulgarity of our flying reality), "Leonardo da Vinci Airport."

To our ancestors, the observation of the hawk's flight, the humming-bird's flight, and the swallow's flight was the vision of an impossible dream. "If I were a bird and had two wings, I would fly to you," says a popular song, a song that is impossible to be sung today with any honesty. Our ancestors projected the myth of flying onto birds, and they did it spontaneously, because birds were at the origin of the myth. But we can no longer do it, because our reality of flight has overcome the flight of birds without having overcome the myth, and this is the illustration of the second difficulty.

Therefore, we can no longer experience the flight of birds as our ancestors experienced it. But this inability of ours paradoxically allows us to see, even better than our ancestors, what the flight of birds represented to them. Maybe they believed that "to fly like birds" is to see the world from above and to go over unwinnable obstacles. Therefore, distance and freedom. However, this type of "sublimation" and freedom does not attract us: we know its reality. There is, however, another charge to the dream "to fly like a bird" that our ancestors felt but that did not stand out clearly: to overcome bi-dimensionality. The fact that we are prisoners of bi-dimensionality is not clearly recognized. We have the illusion that our movements occur within the three dimensions of space. However, in reality, our terrestrial condition condemns us to the plane (the surface of the Earth). Only our hands allow us an opening to the third dimension, to the "conception," "apprehension," and "manipulation" of bodies. To fly like birds is to be able to use the whole body as if it were a hand, to be able to move oneself entirely within the space. This is the aspect of the myth of flight that becomes visible after we have realized the aspects of "elevation" and "the overcoming of barriers."

If we observe the flight of birds, we are in the presence of bodies that move freely within the three dimensions of space, and that assume three dimensional attitudes in all their gestures. Not only is "to go up" and "to go down" equivalent to "to go back," "to go forward," "to go right," and "to go left," but also "to bend the wing" is equivalent to "to turn the corner." We are in the presence of beings that must make decisions, in every given situation, between a much greater number of alternatives than terrestrial beings: the diagonals that offer themselves as lines of flight or attack to birds do not form circles, but spheres. A bird in flight is not the center of a vital structure of interferential circles as a terrestrial animal is, but rather of interferential spheres. The formations of migrating birds obey the rules of three-dimensional geometry and their "mysterious" sense of orientation is mysterious to us because they orient themselves within the three dimensions of space. "To fly like a bird" would mean to be able to move, decide, organize, and orient oneself within three-dimensional space.

Terrestrial animals, and more specifically man, are not entirely deprived of an opening toward open space. But the "third" dimension is nothing more than a series of epicycles superimposed over a plane. The movements of the legs, necks and tails are attempts toward the third dimension from the plane. And the senses, more specifically vision, are organs that collect information that come from the three dimensions over a point on the plane. For terrestrial animals, including man, space is an ocean that bathes the flat island they inhabit. Hence the similarity between birds and fish: they are both inhabitants of an ocean-space. Birds swim in the air, like fish fly in the water. The difference is that the bird's flight highlights the freedom of special movement, and the way the fish swims highlights its conditioning. The myth of the fish has a different climate than the myth of flight.

Man distinguishes himself from other terrestrial animals by his erect posture: his entire body is an advance toward open space. This posture allows man to "conquer space" from the plane. (The bird does not need to conquer space, it is already in it.) However, the erect position of the human does not result in the freeing of the whole of the human body toward space. It only expanded the parameters for three-dimensional movements of several parts of the body, and allowed the hands to manipulate bodies three-dimensionally.

Hands are specifically human organs, made possible thanks to the erect posture, and they move within space with relative freedom. Hands live within a climate structurally similar to that of birds in flight. A bird in flight is a flying hand, a hand free of a body, a body turned into a hand. The movement of our hands means apprehension, comprehension, conception, and modification of bodies "in depth," that is, in space. The myth of flight is this: freedom to apprehend, comprehend, conceive, and modify in depth.

For our ancestors, the bird was the link between animal and angel. It is not an angel yet, because it is still subjected to the Earth's attraction. It takes off from the Earth, concentrates its interest upon the Earth, returns to the Earth, and builds its nest upon it. It is a hand linked to the body of the Earth by an invisible arm. An angel is extraterrestrial. It concentrates its interest upon space and lives in space. It is a hand free of a body: the myth of the spirit-dove. An angel is a being that apprehends, comprehends, conceives, and modifies "freely": pure spirit. A hand free of a body is pure spirit. The bird's flight is its model.

Jet flights from São Paulo to Paris overcome Leonardo's dream, but they do not reach the "freeing" dimension of the myth of flying. They are made from bi-dimensionality: they link two cities in a flat map. The jet flights from Tokyo to Paris link two cities through the polar route and impose a new, flat projection onto the globe. They are more "spiritual" because they demonstrate the projective character of the plane, but they are still made from the plane. However, the experiments of Skylab point beyond the bird toward the angel. The astronauts that live in zero-gravity and space-walk seek to transform their bodies into hands. A phenomenological description of their experiences is missing and would be very revealing. Cassiano Ricardo has, in this sense, a poem entitled "Gagarin." But the Marxist dictum persists: dreams are killed once realized. To become a bird, to become a hand, and to become angel is to kill bird-ness, hand-ness, and angel-ness. Because the dream of freedom and of the sublime, once realized, reveals conditioning as the contradiction of freedom, and the everyday as the contradiction of the sublime. This refers not only to astronauts ("technological angels"), but also to communist society ("society of angels"). Myths are realizable and killable, but they will persist as dead weights after having been realized.

We cannot experience the flight of birds as our ancestors experienced it: as an impossible desire. We experience their flight as a realizable desire, already partially realized, and partially on the way of being realized in dimensions only vaguely dreamed by our ancestors: bird flight as distance, as the overcoming of barriers, and also as spiritualization through three-dimensionality. But as we experience flight as a realizable dream, we are demystifying the desire without freeing ourselves from the myth. We can no longer have impossible desires. What is left for us is the impossible desire of having impossible desires. Is this an apocalyptic vision, or a vision that is integrated to our own vision of birds in flight?

Rain

The observation of rain through a window is accompanied by a sensation of coziness. Out there, the elements of nature are at play and their purposeless circularity turns as always. Whoever is caught in its circle is exposed to uncontrollable forces, a powerless part of its violent gyrations. In here, different processes are at play. Whoever is inside directs the events. Hence the sensation of shelter: it is the sensation of one who is within history and culture contemplating the meaningless turbulence of nature. The drops that hit against the window, projected forth by the fury of the wind but incapable of penetrating the room represent the victory of culture against nature. When I observe the rain through a window, I not only find myself out of the rain, but also in a situation opposed to it. This situation characterizes culture: the possibility of a distanced contemplation of nature.

However (and unfortunately), this is not what we have in mind when we speak of the conquests of culture: to be seated in a dry and warm place, contemplating the cold rain, smoking a pipe, and listening to Mozart. Unfortunately, we have in mind things such as, how "to control the rain." We pretend to change the structure of natural events, to break with their circularity, to make them run linearly, in search of a purpose chosen by us. Rain, no longer as a phase of the eternal circulation of water, but as a phase of a deliberate irrigation of my field. If the rain had been won, it would no longer fall as it does now ("September rain, of every September as always"), but as "this afternoon's, programmed, four o'clock rain." It would be a historical rain, because it would be subjected to a program, therefore part of culture and not of nature. Seen from the window, such rain would not distinguish itself from the rain that is falling now, however, it would be falling on this side, and not on the other side of the window of culture.

This gives us the chills. It seems to be the same rain, but it is not because it is "culture"? Not for being different, but for having a different structure: the linear structure of history, and not the circular one of nature? And it shall not suffice to look at it in order to know this? What a terrible thing! I cannot distinguish between culture and nature looking at things, but only by learning about them. If I look through a window and see rain, chairs, and trees, I cannot know which of these things are culture and which are nature. I depend on others to tell me.

I cannot accept this. If this were true, I would no longer have my own criteria for any type of engagement. The French Revolution would become a historical phenomenon according to *one* explanation and a natural phenomenon (as is the migration of birds) according to *another*. The ones who engaged in it and who died for it, did so naively: they did not collect all the available explanations. I cannot accept that.

I shall return to look at the rain through the window to see if it will tell me something about itself. Here is what the rain is saying: out here it is raining and in there you are sheltered. This is the categorical distinction between nature and culture. Nature is like the rain: it provokes a sensation of powerlessness. Culture is like the living room: it provokes a sensation of shelter. To conquer nature is not to change its structure, but its climate. But this problematizes human progress as a whole. Would we have "essentially" conquered nature along the course of the last, say, two hundred years, in the sense of having enlarged the field of the sensation of "being sheltered?" Does 20th century man feel more sheltered than the man of the 18th century? Would he be more "cultured" in this sense? Doubtless, the observation of the rain demands that we redefine our engagement with culture.

To break with the circularity of natural events, to make them run linearly in search of purpose, to program them: this is the engagement recommended by technocrats and the establishment. Rain, no longer circular and good for nothing, but linear rain, good for irrigating fields. Here is what the technocrats say: culture is the transformation of something that is good for nothing into something that is good for a deliberate purpose. Culture is the injection of "values" into a set of elements that is exempt of values called "nature." Things are natural (the technocrats say) when they cannot be judged "bad" or "good." And things are cultural when they are "good." That is why the natural sciences are "exempt of values" (*wertfrei*): they deal with things that are exempt of values. And the technocrats go on: the true engagement with culture is the engagement in the production of "goods," that is, of "good" things. The technocrats are mistaken and they are misleading us.

In reality, that which is "exempt of values" (*wertfrei*) is technology - the things produced through technical means. Yes, these are neither bad nor good. The things of nature are all bad, because they condition me and make me powerless. If the things of nature were not bad, the engagement with culture could not be explained: it is always an engagement against nature. Technical things are ethically neutral, and they become good if they shelter me, and bad if they condition me. To produce them is necessary but not enough. It is necessary because it results in potentially good things. But it is not enough, because it may result in bad things if we lose the awareness of culture. If "progress" is, as the technocrats affirm, a process through which natural events are transformed into linear events, then "progress" (and "order") is not enough. What is urgent, so that progress has meaning, is to maintain and refine the critical capacity of values (the ethical and political capacity, in sum: freedom). Technocrats are not enough.

The rain that I observe through the window is bad (and it does not matter that some romantics disagree). It is bad because it falls on me without having consulted me. This is the reason why I feel good as I observe the rain: I oppose myself to it. Rain transformed into programmed irrigation is neither bad nor good (and it does not matter that the technocrats disagree). It is neither bad nor good because its value will depend on that which it irrigates. And it will be good only if that which it irrigates is a thing that shelters me. But if that which the rain irrigates is a thing that conditions me, then the programing of the rain will have produced an evil worse than the evils of nature. Technocrats are not only insufficient, but they may also become dangerous. "Progress," if not controlled by a critique of values, may be more dangerous than any immobilism.

The rain that I observe through the window gives me a good sensation, because I feel free from it. I am sitting in a warm and dry room, and I can contemplate the rain. I can observe it, not only to manipulate it later, but also in order to judge it. I am in a situation that allows for a judgment of values, in a situation of "accessibility" in relation to the rain, in a situation of freedom. I may invite others to enter my room in order to discuss the problem of the rain. Out there it is raining and we, in here, sheltered, are discussing how to manipulate the rain so that it can become good. This is culture. Not the manipulated and programmed rain, but the rain that is subject to free discussion. At bottom, freedom is the only thing that is good. Things are good only inasmuch as they contribute to my liberation. And this is also the measure of culture. Technology is not culture yet. And technocracy (an uncontrolled technological government) is anticulture. In sum: culture is technology plus freedom.

It is the rain that I observe through the window that teaches me this. It teaches me that it is I, and those around me, who confer value and meaning. Culture is not a question of rain (be it controlled and programmed or not), but a question of which sensation it provokes in those who observe it through the window. In other words: if I observe the rain through the window, I see that the only justification for an engagement with culture is to enlarge the field of freedom (to enlarge the room from which I observe the rain). The rain teaches that human dignity cannot be summed up as the struggle against nature. There is, between nature and culture (between rain and room), an ethically neutral but potentially dangerous region, a programing region exempt of values. The region of a non-political establishment (of the technicians of field irrigation). Human dignity also demands that this region be appropriated. But in the current situation it is obviously easier to struggle against nature than to appropriate the establishment. As a consequence, there will always be less natural rain and always more programmed rain, and always less rooms from which any type of rain may be contemplated. If it carries on in this manner, the result will be this: we will all be exposed to programmed torrential rains without interruption, but we will proclaim to the four winds (that will howl around us as a programmed chorus) that we are being irrigated.

The Cedar in the Park

A curious fact: trees are almost invisible. Every attempt to contemplate them proves it. There is a dense, multilayered mist between the one who contemplates and the tree. The mist reflects the light that comes from the lighthouse of contemplative intention; thus, contemplation is surreptitiously transformed into reflection and the one who contemplates cannot interfere in this. There is something that surrounds trees, something that is mysterious because it is nebulous. If I look through my window and seek to contemplate the cedar that rises, majestically, in the center of my Angevin park, I have to accept this fact as the starting point that is imposed upon me by the situation in which I find myself.

To be sure, trees are partially invisible for, shall we say, physical and biological reasons, as their largest part is buried under the ground. Such a mundane and apparently obvious fact tends to be forgotten, however, by many of the thinkers that take trees as structural models (trees are in fact the preferential model). I shall give only one example. There was a worldview and philosophy in the 19th century (the "biologizing" one), which conceived of the world as a process that tends to ramify according to a "principle" that Schopenhauer called "*principium individuationis.*" The Darwinian system illustrates this dynamic structure well, for which the "genealogy tree" served as a model. This worldview and philosophy is a historicism that offers itself as an alternative to the dialectical vision of history, and it emerged, effectively, in opposition to Hegel. However, it is obvious that the model for these systems is not the tree as a whole, but only the part of the tree that is visible above ground. Whoever takes the whole tree as a model for systems must deal with a structure that ramifies in two opposite directions, so that the whole tree is a model for a dialectical system, in the strictest sense of the term. The Darwinian thinkers of the 19th century forgot about the subterranean part of the tree (which obviously does not affect the "truth" of their statements in any way).

However, it is not this "partial invisibility" that stands in a nebulous way, as mentioned, between the tree and the one who contemplates it. What stands between them are phantasms, ectoplasms, specters and ethereal bodies that hover around trees and make them inaccessible. Such arboreal divinities inhabit all mythologies, including the Jewish and Greek ones, these inescapable sources of our view of the world. I will mention some of these phantasms. The closest one to the one who contemplates, and therefore the easiest one to be removed, is the specter of the "lung" that conceals the tree as a concrete phenomenon. I do not see a tree, I see a green lung, and I see this lung both morphologically as well as functionally. A little bit closer to the tree, but also easily removable, is the phantasm of the "shelter." I do not see a tree; I see an umbrella, both in the physical as well as in the metaphorical sense of the term. Other specters hold on to the tree more firmly. For example the specters of "fertility," of the "phallus," and of the "tree of life." When these specters are painstakingly removed, and the essence of the tree seems to want to reveal itself, we verify that it is still not the tree-ness that reveals itself, but some even deeper prejudices that probably do not even have a name. The fact is that the relation "man/tree" is laden with so much immemorial charge (a probable consequence of the human arboreal "origin"), that the attempt to grasp the essence of the tree generally fails. The prejudices are so many that they refuse to be put within parentheses and temporarily removed.

I will not seek, therefore, to grasp the essence of the cedar in my park, but only one of its aspects. This: the strange and foreign climate that it irradiates. Since I shall not grasp the cedar-ness of the cedar, maybe I will grasp something of its strangeness or foreignness? After all, I am just as strange and foreign in my Angevin park as is the cedar. Could not such communion between my own "being-in-the-world" and the cedar's form the basis for an intuitive view? Or am I already anthropomorphizing the cedar? Am I already falling into the trap of one of the specters that conceal the cedar, the "anthropomorphic" trap? Into the trap that the boy from Goethe's *Erlenkönig* fell and died? It seems to be more prudent to seek to grasp the cedar's strangeness in the form of questions, and not of statements. Provocative questions that make the cedar speak, and perhaps, certain answers may be provoked from the cedar.

First question: How do I know that the cedar is a stranger? Answer: I know that tree is a cedar, and cedars are native to Lebanon and are not from France. This answer is no good. It was not given by the cedar, but by my schoolbooks. However, beware. The answer is not entirely impertinent. "Cedars from Lebanon": does this not mean King Solomon and the building of the Temple? And is there not something of this meaning around the cedar in the park? Or is this not one of such specters?

I will reformulate the first question: How does the cedar in the park tell me that it is a stranger? In several ways. Its green is different from the green around it. Its pyramidal and hierarchically scaled "Gestalt" is dissonant with the "Gestalten" of the cone shaped trees around it. The tortured form of its branches, its chaotic element which is nevertheless inserted in its harmonic totality, distinguishes it from the soft treetops that surround it. Its monumental pines are unparalleled among the fruit in the park. Its elephantine trunk sounds like a trumpet in a string orchestra. But, principally, its presence dominates the park, not only due to its greatness, but also by something that must be called "majesty." These are answers given by the cedar itself and must be accepted.

Second question: Therefore, in accepting such answers, how do I know that they mean the cedar's "strangeness?" Do they not, on the contrary, mean an aspect of its "cedarness?" In other words, does the cedar's presence in its native Lebanon have the same climate that it has in the Angevin park? If I formulate the question thus, the cedar falls quiet. Necessarily, because the cedar is here and not in Lebanon, and it cannot speak in the name of "another cedar."

Formulated thus, the question is typically meaningless. I have sinned, for having formulated the question thus, against the first commandment of honesty: "Thou shalt not remove phenomena from their context!" The question must be reformulated in order to be meaningful.

I will reformulate the second question: The questions that the cedar gave to the first question, mean that it distinguishes itself from its context for being a cedar or for being a stranger? The answer that the cedar gives to such a question may be summarized thus: I am a stranger for being a cedar. I am faithful to myself, in my color, in my "Gestalt," in my pinecones; I do not assimilate myself to the park. Hence, that is exactly why I dominate the park. I centralize the park; I give it form and sense. The park is the park that it is thanks to me: a park around a cedar. If it were not for me the cedar, therefore, the stranger in the park, the park would not have any sense. I am the noise in the park that transforms its redundancy into meaningful information. I am in discord, and this dissonance is the nucleus of the park's music. This is the meaning of my answers: I am a stranger for being a cedar, and it is only in relation to my strangeness that the park becomes native. "Being a stranger" is therefore, essentially this: to reveal to the context that it is not itself strange. I am a stranger not in myself, but for the park.

These are very problematic answers. They come formulated within discourses, the origin of which I know well. These are the discourses of existential philosophy, informatics and musicology. May the cedar have recourse to these types of discourse? Perfectly. With effect, it cannot but have recourse to these types of discourses. Because the cedar presents itself to me, and if I allow it to speak, it is so that it speaks within my discourses. In effect, the answers to my first question were also articulated by my own discourse, despite having been apparently more concrete. Only that the discourse of those answers was the one of ordinary language. So that I am also obliged to accept the answers to my second question.

They provoke a third question: If the cedar is a strange and foreign presence in the park because it clashes with the park due to its fidelity to its cedar-ness, how do I know that it is the cedar and not the park that is a stranger? In other words: if being a stranger is a way of being that is relative to another being, is there not reversibility? Is the cedar a stranger to the park and the park to the cedar? One answer imposes itself immediately and spontaneously: I know that the cedar is a stranger and that the park is not, because the cedar is only one tree and the park is many. Such a quantifying answer must be refused however, as should any quantification, for being rational. It must be refused because it does not hurt the essence of strangeness. It was given, with effect, not by the cedar, but by my inductive and enumerative reasoning. I must reformulate my question, and direct it, not at the cedar, but at the park.

I will reformulate the third question: How do I know that the chestnut tree (and with it the whole park) is native to the Anjou, thus dialectically making the cedar foreign? A torrent of answers springs forth from the chestnut tree. Its summery green with a light hint of autumnal rust articulates the first half of September, "in which we are." Its cone shaped crown is an element of, but also the summary of, the landscape's "Gestalt" as a whole. The richness of the chestnuts that it bears is a testament to the omnipresent fertility of the Anjou and of France. The peaceful atmosphere of a temperate climate that it irradiates, rich in vital sap, is the mood of the whole environment; such as it penetrates the pores, lungs, sensations, and even the thoughts of all present here. The Anjou as a whole, France as a whole, are in the aura of the chestnut tree, and it is only necessary to contemplate the chestnut tree with sufficient patience in order to discover the essence of France. The multiple answers that the chestnut tree gives to my question may be summarized thus: I am native for being a chestnut tree, and I am a chestnut tree for being native, and there are no problems in this. I do not need to affirm my chestnut tree-ness, nor even be faithful to it. All of this is happening through me, around me and because of me, naturally and with the utmost spontaneity. And this is, possibly, an aspect of "nature": to be thus, spontaneously, and without a problem. The chestnut tree (and the whole park) is Angevin nature. And, in contrast to this, the cedar is not nature, but Angevin culture. It is culture, because it affirms itself, is faithful to itself, and gives sense to the whole park. In sum, it is strange and foreign.

This is a surprising answer. (I must confess that it surprised me for having been formulated in the course of this essay. I did not expect it.) The chestnut tree's answer provokes a redefinition of the concepts "nature" and "culture" in different terms from the customary ones: Nature as my spontaneous circumstance, exempt of problems, and culture as a strange and foreign presence in my circumstance, which is self-affirming, and which therefore gives meaning to nature. This needs to be ruminated upon another opportunity. What matters, in the present context, is this: my previous knowledge (botanical or other), with respect to cedars and chestnut trees, does not touch on the subject of strangeness. For example: the chestnut tree may very well be originally from distant forests, and have been imported here, for example, by the Celts. Nevertheless, it is essentially native. The cedar may have adapted itself perfectly to the Angevin circumstance, and may also grow better here than in its native Lebanon, and grow better than the chestnut tree. However, it is essentially foreign. Prejudices do not hurt essences, which are only revealed through contemplations of my park, such as this one. An aspect of strangeness has just been revealed.

Thus: strange (and foreign) is whoever affirms their own self in the world that surrounds them. In this manner, one gives meaning to the world, and, in a sense, dominates it. But dominates it tragically: one does not become integrated. The cedar is a stranger in my park. I am a stranger in France. Man is a stranger in the world.

Cows

Cows are efficient machines for the transformation of grass into milk, and if compared to other types of machines, they have an unquestionable advantage in this regard. For example: they are self-reproductive, and when they become obsolete, their "hardware" can be used in the form of meat, leather, and other consumable products. They do not pollute the environment, and even their refuse can be used economically as fertilizer, building material, as well as combustible fuel.[1] Their care and handling is not costly and does not require highly specialised manual labor. While they are structurally complex systems, functionally they are very simple. Since they are self-reproductive, and since their construction happens automatically without the need of intervention from engineers and designers, this structural complexity is an advantage. They are versatile, because they can also be used as energy generators and engines for slow vehicles. Although they

---

[1] This essay was written during the late 1970s, therefore data regarding the polluting effects of the methane gas emitted by the world's bovine herd was not yet available or taken into consideration. [TN]

have certain functional disadvantages (for example: their reproduction requires anti-economical machines, "bulls," and certain functional problems require the intervention of expensive university specialists and veterinarians), they could be considered as prototypes of future machines that will be designed by advanced technology and informed by ecology. In effect, we may state that, as of now, cows are the triumph of a technology that points to the future.

If we take into consideration their "design," our admiration for the inventor of the cow grows even stronger. Although it is a highly automated machine, controlled by an internal computer (a brain), and although a cybernetic system made of highly refined electrical and chemical pulses guarantees its functionality, the external shape of the machine is made to be quite aesthetically satisfying due to a surprising economy and simplicity of elements. The impression the cow gives is that of a creation that is well-integrated with itself and within its environment. The cow's "designer" was not influenced by this or that contemporary aesthetic tendency, although he did follow an aesthetic intuition characteristically his own (though we can find certain undeniably baroque elements in the cow's design, despite the fact that it betrays the influence of certain 19th century biologizing tendencies). For example: the elegant mobility of the tail contrasts with the solid immobility of the rest of the creation, and generates a tension achieved otherwise only by Calder and his followers. But what is most impressive in the cow's design is this: the surprising gamut of variations that its prototype allows. The prototype is fundamentally simple (it has been elaborated, for example, by Picasso in the *Tauromaquias*), but such simplicity allows for a large number of varied stereotypes. In this respect, the cow's prototype is an authentically open creation. There are, among the stereotypes, the ones that adapt themselves to national and even regional mentalities (Swiss, Dutch, English), the ones that are adapted scenically (cows from the Alps, the meadows, the steppes), and even cheap stereotypes aimed at underdeveloped peoples (Zebu, Central-African cow).

This, however, does not exhaust the cow's "aesthetic message." The stereotypes are supplied to the consumer along with an "instruction manual" that is equivalent to an invitation to take part in a game. The buyer of cows can, if he so desires, project his own model by "crossbreeding" in such a way that the purchase of cows does not condemn him to passive consumerism, but opens space for an active participation in the "cow-game." So much so that, finally, game theory has been significantly absorbed by technology. We can foresee a future moment within which technological progress will no longer be the privilege of a handful of specialists designated by the administrative apparatus, but a game in which the "masses" shall actively participate, freely varying prototypes. The cow's inventor has provoked an authentic technological revolution, in both a functional and aesthetic sense that opens the horizon to a new "being-in-the-world" of future man. This was achieved by having synthesized the most advanced scientific knowledge and the most refined technological methods with an acute aesthetic sensibility and a clear, structural, cybernetic vision, informed by game theory.

There is no doubt: the cow represents a fundamental "departure."

However, this is not to say that the cow does not also represent a danger and a threat. As cows become cheaper and increase in number (an inevitable process given the impetus for progress), and as other machines of a similar type emerge, there will be a subtle yet profound transformation in the human environment. Current machines, to which humanity has been adapting itself through an arduous process since the Industrial Revolution, will be gradually substituted by machines of the "cow" type. And since such machines impose a different vital rhythm and a whole different praxis, there will emerge the need to readapt which will necessarily have, as a consequence, a new individual and collective alienation. This fantasy predicts not only the dissolution of great cities and the formation of small clusters around cows (to be called, for example, "villages") but also, as a consequence, the dissolution of the basic societal structure and its substitution for another that is currently only imaginable. However, that is not the worst of it.

It is well known that humans have the tendency to "mirror themselves" in their products. The process goes roughly like this: man projects models in order to modify reality. Such models are taken from the human body. For example: the weaver's loom has as its model the human finger, and the telegraph is modeled on the human nervous system. The model is realized as a product. Subsequently, the human model behind the product is forgotten and the product establishes itself, in its turn, as a model for human knowledge and behavior. For example:

steam engines are taken as models for the man of the 18th century, chemical factories in the 19th century and cybernetic apparatus today. Such tragic feedback between man and his products is an important aspect of human alienation and self-alienation.

Therefore, the gradual substitution of current machines for machines of the "cow" type, could result in the definition "man = cow." Man may not recognize his own project in the cow, he may forget that the cow is the result of his manipulation of reality according to his own model, and accept the cow as something that is somehow a "given" (for example: he may accept the cow as some kind of "animal" and therefore, as part of "nature"). In this case, the cow will assume ontological and epistemological autonomy and will, so to speak, become a model for humanity itself behind man's back. In being precisely such a highly sophisticated and anthropomorphic machine (by the way, every machine is anthropomorphic for the reasons stated above), the "machine" essence of the cow could become obscured. In such a case, "genetic explanations" of the cow that prove it is a result of human manipulation will be of little use. Through daily contact with the cow, the impact will be at an existential level. At this level, all "explanations" will become irrelevant (just as such "explanations" are currently irrelevant for those who have daily contact with computers). The mere daily presence of the cow will exert its "cowifying" influence. The fantasy refuses to imagine the consequences of this.

However, it is necessary to face the danger. The fantasy must be forced. It reveals the vision of a humanity transformed into a herd of cows. A humanity that will graze and ruminate, satisfied and unaware, consuming the grass in which an invisible "shepherd" elite has a vested interest and will thus produce milk for this elite. The elite will manipulate humanity in such a subtle and perfect manner that humanity will imagine itself to be free. This will be possible thanks to the automatic functionality of the cow. The illusion of freedom will perfectly obscure this "rustic" manipulation. Life will resume itself in the typical functions of the cow: birth, consumption, rumination, production, leisure, reproduction, and death. This is a paradisiac and terrifying vision. Who knows: as we contemplate the cow, are we contemplating future man?

However, the future is only virtual. There is still time for us to act. Progress is not automatic, but a result of human will and freedom. Progress toward the cow can still be stopped, although certainly not as a "reactionary" act, nor through the attempt to deny the obvious advantages of the cow and the imaginative creative force that manifests itself in it, but rather through the attempt to adapt the cow to real human necessities and ideals. The cow is without a doubt a threat, but also a challenge. It must be confronted.

Grass

In front of my house, the grass grows. Is that not curious? I mean the verb I chose in order to say that there is grass in front of my house: is it not curious? Why do I not say that in front of my house there also grow ants and a cat? And why is there no verb that describes the specific occurrence of grass in front of my house? Why can I not say "it grasses" as I would say "it rains" or "it snows?" And if I say that there is a lawn in front of my house, would I be stating something structurally identical to the statements that there is also an anthill, or there is rain, in front of my house? Obviously, the Portuguese language has a way of imposing specific forms onto my thought that makes me grasp the phenomena of the world through specific aspects of such forms. I grasp the grass as something that grows, which is something essential to the grass. In the case of ants and cats, their growth is graspable as an accident. And I grasp the grass as an element of a collective (lawn) that is essentially different from collectives of the "anthill" and "rain" types. I place my trust in the "wisdom" hidden in language: I believe that language "knows" because it imposes these forms onto my thought. I believe that the "essence" of grass is revealed to me as "growth," and as an element of a specific type of collective, through the forms of the Portuguese language. I am obliged to believe this. Otherwise I would fall into silence or into linguistic eccentricities of this type: "There is an army of grass stationed in front of my house." But as I say this, I trip over the path of my discourse. What kind of linguistic eccentricity was this? Is it not the case that the stationed army of grass also grasps an aspect of the "essence" of my lawn, an aspect hidden by everyday language? And could this not have something to do with the "revealing power of poetry?" Have I not, accidentally, just given the word to the grass in a Husserlian sense, that is: to give a "new" word to grass? Have I not just allowed the grass to articulate itself to me in a relatively new Portuguese way? I shall give neither a positive nor a negative answer to such a question at this point. I shall only register the question.

In front of my house, the grass grows. Just as further on wheat grows. Just as a branchy cedar grows, in the center of the scene that I see from my window. Would "to grow" therefore be the form through which language grasps the essence of plants? Error. The grass in front of my house grows a lot more like the hairs in my head grow, and a lot less like the cedar grows. The essence of the grass, revealed through language, is not its "plant-ness," but the fact that the grass may be left to grow or that it may be cut. The essence of the grass is its cuttability. It is a species of the same genus to which hair and nails also belong. This is a genus that is essentially manipulated by way of manicures. The acceptable technique for the manipulation of grass is taught in beauty parlors. The way that grass grows is essentially different from the way that the cedar grows (as well as wheat). The criterion for this essential difference is in the praxis. The barber is almost competent to cut the grass, but not the cedar, an essential difference hidden by the verb "to grow" [*crescer*] from the Portuguese language. This must also be registered.

The cuttability of the grass (which is essential to it) is apparently linked to the collective character of which it is an element. Collectives of the "lawn," "head of hair," and "beard" types are cuttable, collectives of the "wheat field" type are harvestable and collectives of the "pine forest" type are manipulable through other means (not to mention collectives of the "anthill" or "clowder of cats" types). But is it not the case that nails are equally cuttable, though "cuttability" is not the "essential" quality of nails? What is the collective noun for nails? The attempt to appeal to the help of the "wisdom" hidden in the Portuguese language fails: the essence of grass is hidden by the verb "to grow," even if we force a link between the verb and the noun "lawn." We must verify, somewhat extra linguistically, that grass belongs, essentially, to the class of cuttable phenomena to which hair and nails also belong, but not wheat, ants, nor cats (even though such classification is made possible through and thanks to language). What is surprising is the fact that this classification does not coincide in any way with the so-called "objective" scientific classifications.

These objective classifications (and the whole of the scientific discourse) tend to conceal the essence of the phenomena that they explain. They say, for example, that grass and wheat are close relatives as well as distant relatives of the cedar, but that its proximity to ants is very remote and that its relation to hair and nails is hierarchically confusing. This is due to the fact that scientific objectivity is, in reality, the result of a specific point of view of the world, one assumed subconsciously by a preference without explicit justification, and accepted subconsciously. Certainly, the scientific point of view cannot be assumed by God, "*sub specie æterni.*" From such a point of view, cuttability reveals itself as the essence of several other collectives: of pine woods, anthills, and humanity. We are, from this point of view, essentially as cuttable as grass. If we assume such a distanced point of view, it is not only humanity which reveals itself as a kind of lawn, but the whole biosphere becomes a kind of cuttable moss that covers the surface of planet Earth. Such a distant point of view, however, is neither scientific nor existentially relevant. Only distances that are measurable in temporal and special units compatible with human dimensions are existentially meaningful. Points of view in which the differences between lawn and humanity are diluted are inhuman and therefore sinful – an argument that may be appreciated when set against certain religions.

Grass is essentially the Earth's hair and hair is essentially the body's grass. From which point of view? From the points of view of the barber and of the gardener. These points of view were not assumed arbitrarily; they were imposed by the phenomenon. We cannot assume just any point of view in relation to grass (for example, the point of view of the geologist or the banker). Although these points of view also encompass grass and hair, they do not grasp what is essential to both. For geologists and bankers, grass and hair do not occupy the center of interest; for barbers and gardeners, they do. The essence reveals itself only when the contemplated phenomenon occupies the center of interest.

Grass is essentially the Earth's hair. It is a problem, as is any other phenomena that surround us. The problem of grass is this: to let it grow, or to cut it. It is a practical problem which proves that grass is a concrete phenomenon. It is not a case of explaining it but a case of modifying it. It is not a problem of the "what is the distribution of prime numbers in the natural numbers series?" type because it provokes praxis. Obviously not from an objective point of view, but from the point of view of the gardener. Objectively, the problem of the cuttability of grass will emerge very late in the discourse that explains grass. First, the problems related to morphology, metabolism, genetics, etc. emerge: proof that the objective (scientific) point of view abstracts and de-concretizes the grass. The gardeners' point of view grasps the essence of the grass as a concrete phenomenon. But it is a fact that the gardener can cut the grass scientifically. Science is a long journey that goes through the labyrinths of abstraction in order to reencounter the concrete phenomenon from which it departed. This journey enriches the gardener's concrete praxis (and view). However, when it is a case of discovering the essence of grass (its cuttability), it is better to put this turn within parentheses.

Grass is essentially the Earth's hair. The decision to let it grow or to cut it depends partially on the cultural situation in which we find ourselves. It is partially a question of fashion. "Beautify America, have a hair cut," also implies: "you may or may not cut your lawn."

"The greening of America" is a vision of America from the gardener and barber's point of view. This point of view may be found, as a matter of fact, in many speculations of the New Left (Marcuse) and of a "philosophy" inspired by ecology. There is an implicit aestheticism in several of these new trends, because such trends are born in beauty parlors. For the New Left, the proletariat, the bearer of the future, is apparently not the metal worker, but the barber. Is this aestheticism effectively new? Or is it Romantic, with long beards (and lawns)? This was an impertinent critique. Anything that is new has, in a way, a long beard. "*Nil novi sub sole*." But let us not forget that the essence of the beard is its cuttability. To let the grass grow, to not cut it, is currently in fashion. They say that humanity's survival depends on this. Down with the grass cutting apparatus, because down with every apparatus! The barber's point of view (or the anti-barber, which is the same thing) challenges the apparatus' point of view (that of the worker and the owner of automobile and lawn mower factories). Long beards, from both points of view, are, however, cuttable, as is the long beard of the contradiction between the ethical point of view of the lawn mower factory and the aesthetic point of view of the gardener. Whoever cuts beards in such a way transcends fashions (is transmodern). Structuralist? Yes, but a structuralist-barber that needs to cut his own beard. To cut one's own beard: a reflexive praxis?

Grass is essentially the Earth's hair. To let it grow is to let the Earth be. This is a Chthonic, Telluric, etc., attitude, contrary to the uranic repression (spiritual) of the Earth, exerted by the apparatus (lawn mower). Hair is essentially the body's grass. To let it grow is to let the body be: an attitude contrary to the repression of the body by the apparatus. The body-Earth: a non-historical whole in revolution against a history promoted by the spirit-apparatus. Rousseau-Marx-Marcuse? Not fundamentally. Fundamentally: beauty parlor. A Nietzschian aestheticism in rebellion against a Judeo-Christian "nihilism." It urges us to better define the relation between grass and Earth and between hair and body, in order to phenomenologically discover the Earth behind grass and the body behind hair. Grass and hair "cover" Earth and body. It is because of grass and hair that we do not see them. Is grass even Earth (*Magna Mater*, uterus etc.), and is hair even body (a set of concrete experiences and gestures)? No, because grass and hair are essentially cuttable and the Earth and body essentially non-cuttable. The Earth is not cuttable because it is fundamental. The body is not cuttable because it is always present with me. The Earth and the body are not cuttable because they are not in time. Hence their non-historicity. To let grass and hair grow is still a historical decision (spiritual, set in the apparatus): it is to leave the non-historicity of the Earth and of the body covered. Maybe the opposite method is more advisable? To cut grass and hair so radically that the Earth and the body emerge? To make the apparatus function to the point where it becomes absurd? To see the barber as the proletarian bearer of the future, in the sense of being "the revealer" of the non-historical concreteness of the Earth and the body? Or would this be to collaborate with the apparatus and be absorbed by it? No: it is to appropriate the beauty parlor.

The shortcomings of the "wisdom of language" in relation to grass have been appropriately registered. Language is a part of the grass cutting apparatus. It is possible to transcend language and the apparatus. The phenomenological view allows for it. Afterwards, however, it is again necessary to resort to language and apparatus in order to force them to function against themselves in favor of the essence of grass: a reasonable program.

Fingers

I try to observe them as they hit the keys of the typewriter in order to produce the present text. It is a hard task, because it is a complex situation. I must observe my fingers as they write a text whose subject is the observation of those fingers. It is a passionate task, because the complexity of the situation owes itself to the constant mirroring of the observation in the observed. It is, therefore, a complexity of reflexive situations. As I observe the fingers, I reflect myself in them, and they reflect themselves in me while being observed. When I concentrate my interest upon fingers, I find myself in that center. I am my fingers and my fingers are me. I am theirs just as much as they are mine. Is the essence of fingers perhaps the co-implication of my fingers and me?

In order to overcome the complexity of the situation I shall seek to describe it in simple terms. I am sitting on a chair. The chair is a product of Western civilization and if it were to be analyzed it would reveal the history of the West. I am facing a writing desk. The desk belongs to the same set of which the chair is a part. The juxtaposition "chair – desk" is a characteristic structure of particular situations of my culture. On the desk there is an Olivetti typewriter. This is a slightly paleo-technological writing instrument (a product of the beginning of the 20th century). The machine has keys inscribed with letters of the Latin alphabet. These letters are historical modifications of symbols that originated in the Middle East approximately three thousand years ago. My fingers hit the keys in a particular order. The order seeks to produce sentences of the Portuguese language onto the paper leaf inserted in the machine. This order is therefore determined by the specific order of such language. Portuguese is a historical modification of a hypothetical Indo-European tongue. The Portuguese sentences sought by my fingers are articulations of my thoughts. These thoughts were programmed by the economic, social, and cultural (in sum, historical) conditions that determine who I am. I seek to detach the paper from the machine once it is ready, so that it may be read by an-other. This other will be able to decipher the message on the paper as he or she participates in the same culture as I do. The whole situation, then, is characteristic of a particular culture. My fingers are inserted in it.

But does this allow me to consider my fingers as if they were an integral part of that culture? It does not. The analysis of my fingers will not reveal the history of the West, as the analysis of the chair, the machine, the alphabet and the Portuguese language will. To be sure: the gestures of my fingers on the machine may, if analyzed, be revealed as a historically determined gesture. But not the fingers: they are not the products of the history of culture. I am strongly tempted to say that they are the products of the history of nature. I have very strong models (the

Darwinian for example) that allow me to say this. And to say, therefore, that my fingers are natural phenomena that were introduced into a cultural situation, which thus transforms, informs, or in sum – that conditions their gestures. Culture as the violation of nature.

Such a description of the situation would be, however, entirely inappropriate. It would not grasp its climate. Such climate is not that of the violation of my fingers by a cultural establishment, made up of synchronized apparatus (even though several current trends, including the New Left, believe that it is so). Within this situation, it is not a case of a "denaturalization" or "acculturation" of my fingers. An observation of the fingers' gestures proves that this is not so. They do not move mechanically, although they move within and upon several "machines" (the one for writing, the alphabet, the Portuguese language). Their movement is deliberate, that is, they articulate my freedom. The fingers choose particular keys and ignore others, and they choose each key according to criteria. It is true that the criteria are imposed upon the fingers: by the order of the keyboard, by the rules of language and by the structure of my thoughts. But these criteria make possible, and give meaning to, the fingers' movements; that is, they open a field of choices. My fingers are free within the situation described, with all of the dialectic of freedom that the analysis of the situation reveals. In other terms: the situation is cultural, and thus a field of freedom for my fingers. To formulate it paradoxically: culture is natural for fingers, and outside it, they are not as they "ought to be": free.

What are fingers like outside of culture, and therefore not violated, not appropriated by established apparatus? What is the natural movement of fingers? Their repertoire is reduced. They rub, scratch, maybe point and stab; they hold on to furry objects. These movements are observed in newborn babies, and also in primates. Yes, these are conditioned movements. These are, in thesis, perfectly explainable by the natural sciences. They reflect internal body conditions (thermodynamic and chemical tensions, genetic information, etc.) and environmental conditions. Fingers are entirely determined within natural situations. This late Romantic "revolution," which seeks to free fingers from being violated by the apparatus (for example, through the "pleasure principle"), seeks, in reality, to reduce them to scratching movements. The real revolution would not be to take fingers away from apparatus, but the appropriation of apparatus by fingers. The situation described here, in which I write the present text, may serve as a model to all the cultural situations after such an appropriating revolution. That is why it must be reconsidered.

The typewriter was made in order to serve as a tool for my fingers. It is an extension of my fingers. But it is clear that the relation "machine – fingers" is not simple but dialectic, and that is why it is easily reversible. In order for the fingers to make use of the machine, I must learn how to handle it. I must get to know it. Monkeys can type on a typewriter without knowing it, and if one million monkeys typed on one million typewriters, for one million years they would necessarily produce the present text. Necessarily, but not deliberately. Knowledge of the machine is a presupposition for freedom. Freedom is not an intermediary field between statistical chance and necessity. Such a field does not exist, since statistical chance becomes confused with necessity, and the one million monkeys prove it. Freedom emerges through a dialectic leap, over and above chance and necessity; a leap made possible through knowledge. Without knowledge, the typewriter is not a thing of culture, but a natural condition, as it is for monkeys. There are several, apparently cultural, situations in which we handle apparatus as if we were monkeys, because we are either partially, or entirely ignorant of them. Apparatus and our fingers function within these situations. And it is against these functional situations that revolutions arise: in order to free fingers.

In order to know the typewriter, our fingers must learn to handle it, either empirically or by "*ad hoc*" techniques. That is, they must learn to make movements that are appropriate to the machine, and in this sense, be appropriated by the machine. But this is not an alienating appropriation. It is a dialectic process in which the fingers appropriate the machine as the machine appropriates the fingers. During this process, several virtualities of both machines and fingers are gradually revealed. To learn this is to verify what can be done with machines and fingers. Or better: what fingers can do with the machine and what the machine can provoke the fingers into doing. The machine and fingers then become the two horizons of a dialectic relation (that of writing) in which one horizon exists for the other. The machine exists for fingers (it is made for them), and fingers exist for the machine (they move appropriately for it). But the relation between machine and fingers is not symmetrical (in the sense of when the situation of writing becomes alienating, as in the case of typists in offices and banks). The relation is not symmetrical because the finger's movements – which articulate freedom – determine the machine's movements.

This lack of symmetry cannot be objectively observed. A Martian, when observing a writing process that involves monkeys, typists, and myself, would not notice the difference. Even if all three situations were to be carefully observed, he will only observe the dialectic between chance and necessity, and never freedom. Only I can observe this situation, in which I write and simultaneously transcend it. I do not transcend it as the Martian does, from a distance. I transcend it as a participant: not "metaphysically" but by being engaged. I engage in the situation through my fingers, and transcend it by observing the fingers that are mine. I know, thanks to such transcendence, that I am writing what I want, and not by chance, as the monkeys do, nor according to what I am told, as the typist does. The knowledge of my free will is invulnerable to sophistic argument, even though I also have knowledge of the total determination of my writing act, and of my decision to do it. This is the dialectic of *my* conscience and the Martian will never be able to observe it. That is why freedom cannot be explained, and when it is explained, it ceases to be freedom. However, *I can* concretely observe the fact that I am writing freely. This is the fact that is the aim of every true revolution.

My fingers are unquestionably free within the described situation, but this fact cannot be described.

On the contrary, in pointing to the forces that determine the movement of my fingers, any explanation of the situation will conceal the notion of freedom. Every explanation will reveal that the cultural and natural situation in which I find myself, through my fingers' mediation, defines me completely by determining my fingers' movements. Any explanation is, therefore, an excuse for those who defend situations that are alienating. However, curiously, it is the same for their contesters. The defenders will say that freedom does not exist, that it is a prejudice, and thus they justify the alienating and determining power of the apparatus (be it technocraticly, politically, or traditionally consecrated). The contesters will recommend, it is true, the abolition of determining apparatus through methods that evoke the monkeys' fingers furiously typing the keys until they are destroyed. They want to free typists by transforming them into monkeys. Even though there is, thus, an apparent contradiction between defenders and contesters, there is, effectively, collaboration between them. Chimpanzees collaborate with gorillas because both agree that there is a contradiction between the cultural and natural conditioning of man. Only the defenders of alienating situations opt for the conditioning of culture, and the contesters for the conditioning of nature. But this contradiction between culture and nature does not necessarily exist. Culture may come to be man's nature. In effect, it already is, within particular situations, such as the one just described. And culture, as man's nature, is the field of freedom. In it, fingers may realize their virtualities. This is what the observation of my fingers reveal as they type the present text.

The Moon

Until recently, the Moon belonged to the class of things that are visible, but inaccessible to our hearing, smell, touch or taste. Now, some men have touched it. Has this made the Moon less dubious? Descartes states that we must doubt our senses because, among other reasons, they are mutually contradictory. Until now, the Moon had been perceived by only one of our senses. Therefore, there was no contradiction between the senses. Now, such a contradiction has become possible. Thus we may doubt the Moon, but in a different way. For example: how do we know that someone has touched it? By having seen the event on TV and reading about it in newspapers. Images on TV are dubious, they could be tricks. If they also have a subtitle "live from the Moon," they become not only dubious, but also suspect. Whoever says, "it is raining, and that is the truth," says less than one who simply says, "it is raining." As for the newspapers, their credibility is not absolute. Hence we may doubt that the Moon has been touched. But this doubt would be even less reasonable than the following: is the Moon fiction or reality? It is less reasonable, because it is less reasonable to doubt culture than to doubt nature.

If done methodically, to doubt nature is reasonable, because it results in the natural sciences. But apparently, to doubt culture (TV and newspapers) results in nothing. Since the Moon (according to TV and newspapers) has left the field of nature and entered into that of culture, it is better to no longer doubt it. It no longer remains within the competence of astronomers, poets, and magicians, and is now handed over to the competence of politicians, lawyers, and technocrats. And who could doubt them? The Moon is therefore the immovable (although mobile) property of NASA. The Moon is "real estate" = in a state of reality, and any doubts about it have ceased. However, there are still some problems t hat are relative, not so much to the Moon itself, but rather to our own being-in-the-world. These are confusing problems. I shall speak about some of them.

On a clear night, when I look at the Moon, I do not see NASA's satellite. I see a C or a D, or a luminous circle. I see "the phases of the Moon." The Moon changes shape. But I have learned that these changes are only apparent, and that the Moon itself does not change shape. Why are they "apparent?" Is the Earth's shadow not as real as the Moon? Common sense tells me to see change, not of "the Moon itself," but of "my perception of the Moon." The same common sense does not apply to primitive people. They see the Moon rising, setting and rising again. Not only do I see the Moon with my eyes, but also through my culture's common sense, which tells me to see "the phases of the Moon" and not (as yet), "NASA's property."

Would vision be the most common of all senses, more common than common sense? That is: common to all who have eyes? Can all those who have eyes see the Moon?

Photographic cameras and ants? Is it not anthropomorphic to say that the Moon is seen by ants? If I were to build a lens that is structurally identical to an ant's eye, would I see the Moon? Or is there a common sense that relates only to human eyes, which tells humans to see the Moon? Could there be an eye disease in the West that tells me to see "the phases of the Moon," and another more general human disease that tells me to see the Moon?

On a clear night, when I look at the Moon, I do not see NASA's satellite, although I know that what I see is NASA's satellite. I still see the Earth's natural satellite; my vision does not integrate my knowledge. Such a lack of knowledge integration by the sense of vision characterizes particular situations, the so-called "crises." It is probable the Hellenic Greeks knew that the Moon is a sphere, however, they continued to see it as a Goddess. It is probable that the Melanesians know that the Moon is NASA's satellite, however, they continue to see it as a symbol of fertility. In a situation of crisis, our worldview cannot integrate our knowledge.

In order to see the Moon it is necessary to look at it. I do not need to listen to the wind in order to hear it. I may, but I do not need to. In order to see, I need to gesticulate with my eyes and my head, "to lift my eyes to the sky." I need to do what dogs do in order to listen and smell: they gesticulate with their nose and ears. Their world must be different from ours. For us, odors and sounds are *given,* but lights are provoked by the attention (gesticulation) we pay to it. For dogs, odors and sounds are equally provoked. We live in two worlds: one that is given and the other that is provoked by the attention we pay to it. In this sense, sight is similar to touch: it is drawn toward the phenomenon that is to be provoked. The "objective" explanation that eyesight is the reception of electromagnetic wave emissions (just as hearing is the reception of sound waves) conceals the fact that eyes are closer in similarity to arms than to ears. They seek, they do not stand still. This is important with cases such as the Moon, which is visible but not audible. It has been sought, and not passively perceived.

Cultures that do not lift their eyes to the sky, and instead concentrate their attention on the ground (the so called "telluric" ones) do not seek, do not "produce" the Moon. Cultures that spend their time looking at the sky (the so called "uranic" ones) "pro-duce" the Moon, which then occupies an important role in such cultures. The Moon is, in this sense, a "product" of such cultures. How then may I affirm that NASA has transformed the Moon from a natural phenomenon into a cultural one (into an instrument of astronautics) by having touched it, if the Moon has always been a product of our "uranic" culture? In order to answer this question, I must look closer at the Moon.

What does it mean, "to look closer?" It could mean to get closer to the Moon by climbing a mountain or by rocket. It could mean to get closer with a telescope or similar tricks. But this is not what I am trying to get at. Since the Moon is not a given fact, but one that is sought by the attention given to it, "to look closer" could mean to look at it with greater attention in order to see it more clearly. So, if on clear nights I should look at it with more attention, I will understand why I see it as a natural phenomenon. I cannot see it whenever or wherever I want.

Even though in order to see it, I must want to see it, the Moon itself conditions my will. The Moon is provoked by my will to see it; this, however, becomes actualized within the rules of the Moon's game. The Moon imposes the rules of its game onto me. That is why it is difficult to doubt or manipulate it. The Moon is not of my imagination; it is a thing of nature.

My gaze has proven that the Moon is not of my imagination, but it has not yet proven anything in relation to it belonging to nature or culture. Or in fact it has. The Moon is stubborn. It imposes the rules of its own game. I only see where it is because of its own need, a need called "the laws of nature." Cultural things are not as stubborn. They are where they ought to be in order to serve me. If I want to see my shoes, I look in the direction where they ought to be, I see them, and I make use of them. This is the essence of culture. If I want to see the Moon, I am necessarily obliged to look in its direction. This is the essence of nature. That is why I see the Moon as a natural phenomenon, although I know that currently the Moon is no longer where it is by necessity, but is where it ought to be in order to serve as a platform for trips to Venus. I am still unable to see the Moon's utility. I see it as stubbornly useless. I still see it as if it were the Earth's natural satellite.

But my gaze does not give a satisfactory answer to my question. I do not ask why I see the Moon as a natural thing despite NASA, but rather, why do I see it this way despite the fact that it has always been a product of the "uranic" aspect of my culture. Therefore, I do not ask because of my inability to integrate new knowledge, but because of my inability to rememorize origins. I must help my gaze in order to provoke it to answer such a difficult question. Why do I see the Moon as a given, and not as something originally provoked by my culture? The answer starts to articulate itself: it is because I am ambivalent in relation to my culture. On one hand, I admit that my culture is composed of things faithfully waiting to be used by me. On the other hand, I must admit that I cannot be without these things. This is why the Moon is the exact opposite of my shoes. The Moon is necessary, but dispensable. The shoes are deliberate (unnecessary) but indispensable. The Moon imposes its rules over me with its stubborn necessity. The shoes oppress me with their unnecessary indispensability. This is why I cannot see that the Moon was originally provoked by my culture: why would my culture have provoked something that is necessary but dispensable?

My view is deformed by a prejudice which is part of my culture's common sense: all that is necessary and dispensable I call "nature," all that is unnecessary and indispensable I call "culture." Progress is about transforming necessary and dispensable things into unnecessary and indispensable ones. Nature is anterior to culture, and progress is the transformation of nature into culture. When NASA touched the Moon and transformed it into a platform, another step toward progress was taken.

Such a prejudice, which stems from our common sense, is logically contradictory, ontologically false, existentially unbearable, and must be abandoned. And if I manage to push it away, I shall see the Moon more clearly. I see now, surprisingly, that the Moon, far from being a natural phenomenon on its way to becoming culture, is, and always has been, a cultural phenomenon that is starting to become nature. Here is what culture really is: a set of necessary things that become progressively more indispensable. And here is what nature is: a set of unnecessary and dispensable things. Nature is a late and luxurious product of culture. My gaze toward the Moon proves this in the following manner:

For one moment, let us imagine that NASA had really transformed the Moon from nature into culture. This would have been an exceptionally happy case of a "return to nature." We would only need to cut NASA's budget and the Moon would return to being a subject for poets and escape the technocrats' competence. This is Romanticism (from Rousseau all the way to the hippies): to cut NASA's budget. But would this be a "return?" No, it would be an advance. Before NASA, the Moon was a product of Western, "uranic" culture, which had as a projected aim the ultimate manipulation of the Moon by NASA. Our Neolithic ancestors looked at the Moon (and thus "pro-duced" it) with the aim of eventually transforming it into a platform to Venus. And that is what we, their descendants, see when we look at it: a fertility symbol, goddess, and natural satellite. These are several phases on the path toward becoming a platform. We always see the moon as a potential platform, although we do not know it consciously. NASA already existed in germinal form within the first gaze directed at the Moon.

Therefore, to cut NASA's budget would be a step beyond NASA. It would transform the Moon into an object of "art for art's sake," unnecessary, dispensable, to be sung by poets. Such an object we could call a "natural object" in an existentially bearable sense. This transformation of culture into nature happens everywhere: in the Alps, beaches, and in the suburbs of big cities. The 18th century Romantics "discovered" nature (that is, they invented it), and the Romantics of our "*fin de siècle*" are realizing nature. One of the methods of this transformation is called "applied ecology." If this method were applied to the Moon it would become nature. If we were to look at the Moon during clear nights and see it as a natural phenomenon, we would not be seeing the Moon's pre-NASA past, but its post-NASA state. Our vision would be prophetic, that is, inspired by Romanticism. And in effect, this is what we always do: we look at the Moon romantically. This is why we see it as if it were already a natural object, and not what we know it is: the object of a culture that aims to transform it into a platform.

This is a disturbing answer. The Moon is seen as a natural object, that is, as our culture's ultimate product. How then, in such a situation can I engage myself in culture, if it tends to transform itself into its own betrayal, into Romantic nature? This question, however, does not touch the Moon. It continues unperturbed in its necessary and, for the moment, dispensable way. To inquire in this way is of little use. It is useless to lift our eyes toward it. "Lift not your eyes to it, for it moves impotently, just as you and I."[2]

---

[2] This last sentence, which is rendered in English in the original text, is a reference to the *Rubaiyat* of Omar Khayyam (1048-1123). There is one specific quatrain from the fifth edition of Edward Fitzgerald's translation of 1889 that has the same essence of this sentence, however, Flusser summarizes the quatrain but gives no reference. This reoccurs in some of the following essays. [TN]

Mountains

Whoever approaches a mountain range coming from the plains, suddenly suspecting that those nebulous blue forms that popped up on the horizon could be mountains, may nurture the following thoughts: I suspect that these forms on the horizon are mountains, and not clouds, although they seem like clouds, because I know that mountains, if seen from afar, seem like clouds. If I did not know this, the suspicion of seeing mountains would not have occurred to me. Within a few minutes I shall verify my suspicion: I shall see if such forms are mountains or clouds. But let us suppose that I had never seen or heard of mountains: I would obviously have no doubt that the shapes on the horizons are clouds. And in a few minutes, once such forms had revealed themselves as non-clouds, what would I be seeing? Would I not have such an extraordinary and violent experience that it would shock me? A shock that could kill me? He who only knows the plains, where the landscape is always flat, will hardly survive when confronted with something so immensely extraordinary, so gigantically absurd as mountains. The emotions we feel as we approach a mountain range are a pale and late shadow of the sacred terror that our

Siberian ancestors must have experienced as they saw the Pamir mountain range for the first time. (That is, if the hypothesis that we are descendants of the people from the steppe is correct.) This primordial terror must be buried deeply within our collective subconscious.

To look at mountains through eyes borrowed from the nomads of the steppe, is not however, the only way to look at them "without prejudice." The other way is to look at them through the eyes of a mountain dweller that has never left his land. How does someone who knows all the tracks that climb the mountainside and all its fauna and flora see the mountain? Does he see the mountain with the tracks, the animals, and the plants in the same way that we see it? Or does he see tracks, animals, and plants inserted within a general structure called "mountain?" To the extent that what we see is a mountain covered by particular accidents, and what he sees is particular things that relate to each other in the form of a mountain? This is an unanswerable question because we cannot borrow the eyes of the mountain dweller or of the nomad from the steppe. We are condemned to look at the mountains through the lens of our culture's prejudices. We live, as a consequence of this, in a world in which mountains, if seen from afar, seem like clouds.

By admitting that we see mountains through cultural prejudices (as Westerners, Bourgeois, and through the lens of the 20th century), could the mountain dweller and the nomad see without prejudice (naively)? Certainly not. The mountain dweller is conditioned to see them (that is if he does see them, in a rigorous sense) by his culture. And the nomad was conditioned by his culture not to expect mountains, hence their shock. A "naive view, without prejudices" is not a view that is primitive, original, or anterior to culture. It is the view sought by a Western cultural elite, a late product of its millennial development. Naivety is an ideal of a disillusioned culture, an ideal reached by deliberate methods. Non-deliberate naivety is unimaginable; it does not exist (even in children).

But it is still a fact: whoever wants to see mountains as they are, and not as some prejudices make us believe they are, must seek them naively. They must seek to do it deliberately, that is, to look at them not through the eyes of supposed "primitives," but through eyes built especially for naive vision, in the laboratories of specialists in phenomenology. In other terms, if I seek "to allow the mountains to speak, so that they may reveal to me what they are," I am assuming an attitude that was conditioned by a specific and highly sophisticated stage of my culture. This apparent contradiction seems to be inevitable, and does not necessarily invalidate the results that may be reached by a deliberately naive view.

Let us suppose, therefore, that I am a 20th century bourgeois man who approaches the Jura Mountains via the Bourg-en-Bresse road, in order to see them as they are, and not as the tourists see them (tourists being 20th century bourgeois people who approach the Jura Mountains via the Bourg-en-Bresse road in order to see them as they ought to be, according to particular models). My task shall be to attain a deliberately naive view of the Jura Mountains, and this implies the suspension of the prejudices that I nurture in relation to them. However, I may then observe that such prejudices are not necessarily a hindrance in order to see the mountains. They may, on the contrary, become powerful mediations for my view of "mountain-ness." Even more so because they are superficial prejudices that do not seem to touch the phenomenon proper that is the mountain. Effectively, I am verifying this very thing as I approach the Jura Mountains via the road. I nurture several prejudices in relation to the Jura, and some of these prejudices relate to the name (the mere name) of the mountains. As I try to put one of these prejudices into parentheses (a modest task, apparently easy), the following happens:

I remember from secondary school that there is a period in Earth's history called "Jurassic," and that it occupies the central period of the Earth's Middle Ages. I suppose that this name is due to the fact that the rocks of the Jura served for the first excavations of this period (which, if I am not mistaken, is linked to the giant reptiles). This means, therefore, that the mountain range I am beginning to climb was formed during that period, and that the white rocks starting to shine through the trees of the multicolored forest were used in other times by brontosauri to lay their eggs, and by pterodactyls to take off, as today's airplanes do in search of Geneva's airport. (This is only a supposition, as during that time neither lake Leman, nor the Alps, nor even Europe existed in order to be flown over.) This is not a display of knowledge; it is merely a poorly digested information salad from school, superficially assimilated. It is prejudice. And, still, as if by magic, this prejudice has been lifted from the books in order to penetrate the concrete world. I cannot pretend, suddenly, that this prejudice may be diminished when I look at the mountains. And for having remembered it, the pterodactyl is just as present in the mountains as are the leaves of autumn (although they occupy a different level of reality). I could do two things: control my prejudice in relation to the Jurassic Period at the next bookshop in St. Claude, and afterward look at the mountains with a more correct knowledge (although necessarily superficial and scientifically disinterested). Hence, I shall not reach a naive view of the mountains. Or I may attempt to reduce my prejudice, not completely, but in order to reach its essence, which is this: mountains are things that have a history, or, more precisely, a biography. What will happen if I were to look at the mountains through prejudices thus reduced?

This: When I say that these mountains have a biography, I mean to say that they are processes that start with their formation ("birth"), end with their leveling-out ("death"), and that go through stages in which accidents may modify them. They emerge as something new (like newborn kittens or a brand new car), they age, they are used and abused (like a cat that has lost an eye or a second hand car that had an accident), and they disappear from the surface of the Earth (like a dead cat or a recycled car). When I look at these mountains now, I see only one moment of their biography. And now that I assume such a prejudice in relation to them, I see it clearly. The Jura Mountains are in their prime, the Massif Central, which I passed yesterday, are ancient and decrepit, and the Alps on the other side of the lake (whose violent contours I can see) are in full puberty. This is no longer a prejudice: I can now clearly see the phenomenon proper. But this is important: I would not have seen it had I not nurtured those prejudices.

I also see that although the mountain is a process of diachronic structure, similar to that of my car and my hand, there is a difference: my own biography encompasses that of my car's, and it is encompassed by that of the mountain's. My car is an accident in my life, and my life is an accident in the mountain's history. This is therefore not a prejudice: I can see it if I look at my car, my hand and the mountain. I can concretely see that the car is more ephemeral than my hand, and the hand more than the mountain. And I see that this fact has nothing to do with the size and the material of the thing. The car is bigger than my body, but I see that I can outlive it. The car is made of steel, which is more durable than the material of the mountain (not to speak of my body's material), but I see that the mountain will outlive the car. The difference is in the rhythm of the three things (car, hand, and mountain), and I see such difference, as incredible as it may seem. That which we call "life" is a process with a specific rhythm, and that is why I see that the mountain is not a living thing: not because it is not made of amino acids or because it is large, but because it obeys a different rhythm. If I could penetrate this rhythm, I would have access to the mountain's essence. But I cannot.

To penetrate a rhythm means to co-vibrate, to be in "sympathy." This sympathy is considered "knowledge" to the Pythagoreans. They conceived the world as a context of things that vibrate in several rhythms, and knowledge as sympathy with all the rhythms. This knowledge was possible thanks to mathematics and music, because those are the structures of all possible rhythms. If I look at the mountain as I am doing now, I am seeing it Pythagorically: I am trying to discover its essence; that is, its rhythm. But with a difference: I no longer believe that I could reach it mathematically. I know that the mathematization of the mountain will consequently have several strands of the natural sciences, but not the discovery of its essence. That is because mathematics is not the structure of all possible rhythms, but only that of the human intellect. And as for music, I know next to nothing of its efficiency as a method to discover the essence of mountains. Music has never been used for such a purpose along the course of my culture. But I suspect that it has a human rhythm just like mathematics, since it is a close relative. I look at the mountain more or less as Pythagoras did; I feel, just like he did, the mountain's rhythm. But I have lost his conviction that this rhythm is articulated mathematically, and that numbers are the mountain's essence. If to lose convictions is to become naive, then I am more naive than he was. We find ourselves, both he and I, at the two extremes of the process known as the "history of the natural sciences." He ignored everything in relation to pterodactyls, and I ignore everything in relation to the essence of mountains. The history of science is a process along the course of which "essential" knowledge has diminished, and "naivety" increased.

I cannot be sympathetic with the mountain. Hence, this inability of mine is a way through which the mountain reveals itself. It reveals itself as a thing whose rhythm can be felt, measured, even manipulated, but never existentially absorbed. Here is one aspect of the mountain's essence: to be a thing that obeys an ungraspable existential rhythm. Faith may move mountains, and bulldozers may do the same. But nothing is able to grasp its rhythm. There it is, still and silent, passive in its majestic beauty, and now that I have climbed it, I see that its rocks synchronize its diachronicity into parallel layers, transforming "anterior" into "below." I see how it reveals itself under the October sun, through the colorful flames of its forests. I know and feel the pulsation by which it is possessed, but I cannot pulsate with it. It is too different from my own rhythm. This is what I have in mind when I say "mountain": an ungraspable rhythm despite all knowledge. However, if knowledge did not exist, such an essence would not have revealed itself. Had I suspended knowledge, the mountain would have silenced itself in relation to its ungraspable rhythm.

I did not manage to suspend my prejudice in relation to a specific connotation of the name "Jura." Perhaps I did not want to suspend it? Was I right in not wanting to do it? Whoever manages to penetrate deeper into the mountain's essence may answer it: a perfectly viable task through a variety of different methods (all deliberate). As for myself, I shall seek to spend some time in the mountain's bosom. Not as a nomad, or mountain dweller, or child, or tourist, but as someone who cannot and does not want to suspend particular prejudices in relation to the Jura Mountains. As someone who is condemned to live with such prejudices, and sometimes even likes them: another type of naivety?

The False Spring

The landscape that I see when I look through the window is not as it ought to be, and the things out there do not know how to behave. It is mid-February and the landscape should be covered by the coat of winter. The meadows should be asleep, protected by snow. The brooks and the waterfalls should be waiting, frozen still, for the sun's liberating force in March. The pine trees should be laden with their shiny crystal ornaments. The apple trees should seem as if dead, with their contorted branches, bare, clamoring for a rebirth in the shape of flowers and leaves. The bucks and the does should have left their trails on the snow, on their way down to the valley in search of food. The only things moving in the landscape seen through my window should be a few crows in the center of the snow-covered lawn, a few sparrows on the terrace looking for some crumbs, and the neighbor's hairy dog sinking its paws clumsily in the snow. The sky's morning blue should contrast with the shiny whiteness of the landscape, within the transparency of an air that is ten degrees centigrade below zero. That should be the scene. But the one that I see is different.

The meadow in front of my house is of a grayish straw color, but in some places it is possible to see a light green tone, as if it were waking from a troubled dream. On the mountainside the waterfalls run through bare rocks, which the snow left uncovered as it retreated to heights above one thousand two hundred meters. The pine trees are as green as they are in June. The apple trees, when looked at from up close, seem to be covered with hints of buds and early shoots. And the terrace is full of singing birds with blue, red, or yellow chests, and of black and yellow beaks. I do not know the species, but I know that they should be in Africa and not in the Alps. In sum, the landscape is as it ought to be at the end of March. No, I correct myself. If we really were at the end of March, the meadow would be slightly green and the first flowers would be blooming in it. The insects would be flying over the meadow, so that the birds would not be at my terrace, but catching insects. And the pine trees would not be green as in July, but that typical light green of spring. What I see through the window is not spring.

There is no doubt; the description of the view through my window is Aristotelian, but not intentionally so. My landscape imposes Aristotelian categories, apparently overcome by Western thought so many centuries ago, onto the description. If I say that the landscape is as it ought to be, I am talking of justice ("*diké*"). If I say that the things do not know what to do (the meadow, waterfall, pine tree, birds, and deer), I am not anthropomorphizing them. I am seeing them as if they were organs of a live super-organism that is ill ("*cosmos*"). When I am describing the disorder out there, I am talking of rhythm ("*pathos*").

In sum, what I am seeing through my window is "nature" in the sense of "*physis*." What I see is that natural things have difficulty finding their just place in nature, that therefore the situation that I see is not natural, and that is why it is false. The natural situation now, in mid February, is the situation of winter. So what I see is a false spring.

I repeat: I did not choose Aristotelian categories intentionally. How could I have done that? Such categories are not mine. I would never intentionally say that the landscape is not as it ought to be in February. According to my categories, the "ought to be" refers to culture, and nature is exempt of values. So for me, the landscape is not as it ought to be if there was a mistake in the planting of the apple trees. I would never intentionally say that the things do not know how to behave. Within my categories, things do not "know." They obey the rules of the game ("laws of nature") by which they are determined. I would never intentionally say that the spring I see is "false." Within my categories, falseness is the property of sentences, or, in other words, it is an aesthetic aspect of human works. And, intentionally, I would never state that the landscape around me suffers some kind of injustice for having its order disturbed. I would say that there are, in this case, several superimposed and interfering "orders." One of these orders is the rotation of the Earth on its axis ("winter-spring"). Another is the one of the winds, determined, among other factors, by the solar processes. I would intentionally "explain" the situation around me as the effects of warm oceanic winds on the Alpine valleys. Not so probable, but perfectly possible, and theoretically, even predictable. Therefore there is no place for "moral" concepts within my own categories for grasping the situation, such as that of justice.

And I say more: I believe that I know how the Aristotelian categories emerged, why they became prevalent during the Middle Ages, and why and how they were overcome during the Renaissance. I believe that these categories are the result of a particular praxis and of a particular ideology that were characteristic of late antiquity. To be sure: the Athenian artisanal and ideological mercantile and land owning praxis. I believe that these categories continued to be active during the Middle Ages for having been adopted as feudal ideology (ecclesiastic), in order to construct an apology for the (then active) social structure. And I believe that a revolutionary bourgeoisie with different praxes and ideologies then substituted these categories for others. Thus, I know that Aristotelian categories reflect a historically determined human "being-in-the-world" that was overcome long ago, and not a supposed "objective structure" of reality. And, even so, I appealed to them spontaneously as I described the landscape that surrounds me.

I cannot deny that these categories were imposed upon me in some way by the things themselves. The birds on my terrace, fighting for crumbs that my wife put there, "really" suffer for the lack of insects. It "really" is not "natural" that the apple trees should bloom now, since the buds will die with the next fatal cold spell that will cover them with snow again. It "really" is not "just" that the snow should have retreated so high up, because with the next snowfall, layers without substratum will form, causing avalanches to occur. The birds, apple trees, and snow "really" are disorientated. They "really" are deceived and "should be doing" what they are doing. It does not seem to be Aristotle saying this, but the things themselves.

It is obvious that I may avoid the epistemological problem which is emerging and crossing my way and my throat by at least two ways. I could say, in the end, that it is Aristotle who is speaking, and not the things themselves. This is because Aristotle lives in me, very close to the surface of my consciousness, where he sleeps a light sleep, and so he was awakened by the events out there. The oceanic winds that invaded my valley provoked in me an epistemological fallback of more than two thousand years. And I could also say that the birds, apple trees, and the snow in fact do speak through Aristotelian categories, because Aristotle formulated such categories through superficial observations, like mine. But, when observed more carefully and with more refined methods, the birds, apple trees, and snow start to speak through more "advanced" categories. Thus, the categories through which all things speak depend on the attention I pay to them as I describe the landscape: a "superficial" attention (*Aristotelianizing*). Both ways of avoiding the problem are equally "good," and, if analyzed, they may be reductive, one for the other. But they do not satisfy me, and the problem persists.

They do not satisfy me because I cannot believe that the spring I see is "false" if I look at it superficially, or that it becomes a perfectly "normal" meteorological phenomenon if I look at it more carefully. I believe that the situation around me is both things: normal meteorological phenomenon and false spring. And this does not depend on the attention I pay to it; it just so happens that I see a meteorological phenomenon if I look at the situation in one way, and a false spring if I look in another way. I admit that I have several ways of looking at things, and that my gaze provokes different aspects in things. But I cannot admit that my gaze put such aspects there: the birds speak in a language too imperative and intensely expressive for me to admit to that. In this case, it is the birds themselves that demand to be looked at Aristotelically. If I were to mentally transport myself to Brazil, the problem might become clearer.

In Brazil, the rhythm of the seasons is not perfectly articulated. Unlike here, in Brazil there is no essential difference between mid-February and the end of March. So this "*physis*" is less dramatic (Easter is less pathetic), and Aristotle is less plausible. But in Brazil there is, as opposed to here, a dramatic division between night and day, as the duration of night and day does not fluctuate so much along the year. So let us imagine that, in São Paulo, during a particular night, the sun rises at three o'clock in the morning, but in a way that it would be possible to see that it would set again within half an hour. It would not be an impossible happening in the strict sense of the term, only an infinitely less probable happening than oceanic winds blowing in the Alpine valleys. It would be a false morning, even more false than the spring here described, for being less probable, but a happening of the same type. What would happen in such a situation? We would all go crazy, men and things. It would not suffice to say that madness is reasonable, that it is primitive, and that the phenomenon would be perfectly explainable when observed carefully. That there was, for example, a very rare, but theoretically perfectly viable, interference from the Proxima Centauri star on our solar system. That this is, therefore, a normal phenomenon, one that confirms astronomical categories instead of challenging them. An argument like that would not suffice. We would all go mad, in spite of it, because even though the argument may be "true," that morning would still be false.

In the hypothetical case of the false São Paulo morning, the Sun's language would not impose upon us Aristotelian categories (as it does with the false spring), but much older ones. Primordial categories of the type "Rah," and "Aton," and "Marduk," and "Shemesh": solar myths. For having broken such mythical primordial categories, the Sun of the false São Paulo morning would drive us mad. And the wind has not driven us mad simply for having broken Aristotelian categories, rather it has merely disorientated us. Therefore, all categories (mythical, Aristotelian, of modern science, and others) are *our* way of seeing things; historically explainable as products of the dialectics between praxis and ideology. But even so, they are not imposed upon things randomly. On the contrary, they reveal particular layers in things. However, they are curiously revealing. These categories mirror "something" of things, but they do so, all of them, in an approximate fashion. Things may break through all of their categories There may be false mornings and a false spring, and stones may fall in a non-geometric acceleration. In sum: all categories may be "falsified" by things. When this happens, we become disoriented, or we go mad, or we simply elaborate new categories that are equally "falsifiable." And our reaction to the falsifications will depend on the depth of the layers of our consciousness (and of things), in which the categories are found.

We do not live, therefore, in *one*, but in many natures: in a nature that is graspable by the categories of our natural sciences, in an Aristotelian "*physis,*" in a nature that is full of Gods, in a nature created by God. All of these natures are there, outside the window, but also in here. They "really" interfere with one another. And sometimes, one of them predominates. As in this moment, when the Aristotelian "*physis*" predominates for having been broken through by the false spring. It broke through for having been broken through. This is not one more "explanation," but a deposition from a concrete experience.

Meadows

When I observe them, cut out from the compact mass of the forest, forming clearings with dappled light within the mysterious shadow that surrounds them, it is not so much about Heidegger, the glorifier of meadows, that I think of. (And I am not sure if the Brazilian reader is aware that "Heidegger" means "the cultivator of meadows in the forest.") I think mainly of the second verse of the *Metamorphosis*, where the situation of the Golden Age is described: "*sponte sua, sine lege fidem rectumque colebat*," that is, "spontaneously, without law, faith and what is right were cultivated."[3] Read within its context and during high school, the verse is impressive for its beauty and its melody for the elegance of its words, and for the grandiosity of its rhythm. And as for its semantic meaning, this seems to be linked to the last words of the preceding verse: "*quae vindici nullo*" (in the absence of judges). But remembering the verse when looking at meadows, its semantic charge acquires new dimensions. And it is practically inevitable for someone who had "Classical Studies" to remember it,

---

3 This is Flusser's own translation. [TN]

since it is a verse that becomes profoundly engraved in one's mind.

Thinking of the verse in this way, every word acquires an aura of meanings that penetrates the view of the meadow. It deserves to be analyzed. But the decisive word is the last one: "*colebat.*" I doubt that it would be possible today to translate it adequately. We have lost the experience of the verb "*colere,*" although we can still experience two of its derivate nouns: "*cultus*" and "culture." To say that "*colere*" means "to harvest," or "to cultivate," or "to worship," or "to wait for," is to fail to comprehend its climate. Surely: the climate is of agriculture, it is aesthetic and religious, it is submissive, but there is, in such a climate, something else that escapes us. If the verse affirms that our elder mystics "harvested faith and what is right," then it alludes mainly to this "something." The meadow can help us to grasp this something.

The meadow or field in Latin is called "*ager.*" But since "*ager*" and "*actio*" are nouns of the same verb "*agere,*" then maybe it would be better to say that for the Romans, meadows and fields were "fields of action" (that is, battlefields). Battle against which enemy? Against the field itself. The aim was to dominate the field. "Dominate," that is, to submit it to the house ("*domus*"). The one who fought against the field was "*dominus*" ("lord of the house") was "*macho*" ("*vir*"), and fought with "*machismo*" ("*virtus*"). In "virtue" ("*virtus*") of such *machismo* the field submitted itself to the dominance ("*imperium*") of the house ("*domus*"). It was a sexual act ("*actio*") by which the field ("*ager*") became harvestable (agriculture). But not immediately. It was necessary to wait to be able to harvest ("*colere*") that which would grow in the field ("*natura*"). This wait and hope of the master in his imperial and imperious virtue was "*cultus.*" In sum, "*colere*" is the victory, patiently waited for, of the dominating and imperious virtue over nature, which results in culture.

The peaceful meadow that I observe, surrounded by the mystery of the forest, vibrates with the climate of this meaning of the verb "*colere.*" It is peaceful for it is the field of a victorious battle. "*Pax Romana*" is a synonym of "*Imperium Romanum,*" although we have forgotten that pacifism and imperialism were originally confused. The meadow is peaceful for having been dominated by patient virtue long ago. It is difficult for us to intellectually grasp that action and passion, activity and passivity, are two sides of the same attitude; one which transforms nature into culture. Intellectually it is difficult, but it is existentially easy in the contemplation of the meadow. The meadow irradiates the peaceful synthesis of a millennial activity and passivity; that is, it irradiates tamed nature.

In times gone by, dense forests must have covered the mountainsides, which now bear the meadows surrounded by forests. In times gone by, but not always. During the last Ice Age, the mountainsides must have been partially covered by glaciers and partially by tundra. Our forefathers must have hunted reindeer and horses in the tundra. After this period, the forest advanced mercilessly with the retreating ice, but our ancestors did not retreat, even if threatened by hunger with the disappearance of the animals from the tundra. They were not animals, our ancestors, they were "*domini,*" they had virtue, they acted and had patience, they had culture. They did not retreat from the tundra as the animals did, nor did they adapt themselves to the advancing forests, as did the species that now inhabit it. They confronted the forest, courageously and with rectitude: "*fidem rectumque colebat.*" And they confronted it, not because they were obliged to do it: "*sine lege.*" They confronted it because they were people: "*sponte sua.*" Spontaneously, that is, according to their nature as men. It is, therefore, natural for them to have opened clearings in the forest in order to dominate it. In virtue of having been men, it is natural that our ancestors chose [*escolheram*] = "*excolebant*" specific places in the forest in order to transform them into culture, into meadows.

We know approximately how they acted: they advanced against the forest with stone and fire. But the difficulty is to intuit how they made their choices. In order to choose a specific place within a given context, and in order to refuse all other places, it is necessary to go beyond the context, to see it from the outside. The difficulty that we have is to intuit such transcendence in such a "primitive" people, as we presume our ancestors to have been. This is because we tend to compare them with contemporary indigenous people, and we do not even evaluate well how contemporary indigenous people live today. These natives living at a Paleolithic level, as our forest domineering ancestors did, must confront nature through the same transcendence with which we confront it. However, they still do not exemplify the "being-in-the-world" of our elders. They probably represent a regressive way of life, and certainly a way of life that has been superseded by the majority of humanity. Our ancestors, on the contrary, were the *avant-garde* of the army of the human spirit that advanced against nature. Stone and fire were weapons that they invented and developed with a revolutionary aim, and the idea of the meadow to be chosen and cultivated was the fruit of a revolutionary and utopian fantasy, never before imagined. They were not primitive, in the sense of having been less sophisticated in their reflection or in their praxis than the current generations. On the contrary, if we seek to intuit their imagination, their discipline and their rigor of thought and action (for example, if we seek to intuit the mind of the inventor of the bow), we must conclude that their mental capabilities are equivalent to those of our most refined elite.

We have proof of the Edisons among the supposed "hordes" that opened the meadows (ceramics, stone-tools, bone needles). We are obliged to admit there were Einsteins among them (the ones that calculated the trajectory of the arrow and the principle of the wedge). We have proof of their Picassos (the elegance of the ornaments). We are obliged to admit to their Kants (the ones that critiqued the principle of the wedge and the elegance of the ornaments), and their Kafkas (the ones that sought meaning behind such action and passion). We must, therefore, imagine the dialogues around the bonfires in the recently cultivated meadows were more like advanced research and development meetings, and less like the contemporary "*potlatch*" of indians in the Aleutian Islands. Otherwise we will not be able to comprehend the elegance, the functional perfection, and the smooth boldness of the meadows on the mountainsides, that which Ovid calls the "*fidem et rectum.*" And the observation of the meadow will also allow us to penetrate some of our ancestors' religious climate. In fact, this is what Ovid had in mind when he said that our ancestors of the Golden Age "*fidem colebat*" (cultivated faith).

The Ovidian term "*rectum*" does not cause us too much difficulty, because the meadow proves to be in the right, correct, and adequate place. The criterion of "rectitude," which, according to Ovid, our ancestors applied spontaneously, is an economic, technical, pragmatic, and methodical criterion through which our ancestors overcame hunting and initiated agriculture. It is the technocratic criterion that marks the passage from the Paleolithic to the Neolithic, from the Golden Age to the Silver Age. (However, Ovid probably did not exactly have this in mind, because "*rectum*" for the Romans is part of the triad "*pulchre, bene, recte*" ("beautiful, good, correct," which therefore implies the notion of truth.) Yet be that as it may, we may agree with Ovid that the observed meadow confirms that one of the criteria of choice in the transformation of nature into culture was that of the adjustment to the economic aims sought. The proof of this is that the meadows continue to function economically up until today, and that the mountain farmer lives very well off of them, as did our ancestors. The problem, and I repeat, is that of the meaning of the second criterion, which Ovid calls "*fides*."

But if consulted, the meadow gives us the answer. Although we know that it is a product of culture, and although we may intuit, discover its "*Gestalt,*" and in its small details, the human hand and spirit, we cannot deny that it is an integral part of nature. Furthermore: the experience of the meadow, of its grass, of its flowers, of its insects, and even of the cows that graze on it, is one of the most intense experiences of nature that we can have, and to lie down on a sun-drenched meadow is to commune with nature. Such an experience is not easily explainable. For example, it cannot be explained by saying that the meadow emanates an intensified climate of nature for having been conquered so many thousands of years ago, and that an industrial city-borough emanates a climate of anti-nature for being a recent conquest. This does not explain the experience, because the vegetable-garden around the farmer's house on the meadow is equally old but does not give us the impression of being nature. It is neither its age, location, flora and fauna, nor even other aspects of the same order that make it so that the meadow, as culture, becomes intensified nature. Rather, it is the criterion according to which it was chosen in order to no longer be forest and become meadow. In fact: "*fides.*"

In virtue of being men, our ancestors had "*fides;*" that is, they were faithful unto themselves, to their own nature, and to the nature that surrounded them. They were thus spontaneously, without either dogma or ideology ("*sine lege*"). They lived according to and in accord with themselves and the world in which they were: the Golden Age. This was their religiosity ("*fides*"): to be faithful to what I am and to what surrounds me. However, this fidelity is not, as we tend to think, "the adoration of primitive nature." It is not a surrendering ("*super-stitio*") to the forces of nature. Such surrendering is not natural to man, and, therefore, it is not fidelity to human nature. To be faithful to oneself, for man, is to go against nature; it is to use the criterion of "*rectum.*" Nature is not as it should be, and must be rectified: this is the attitude of fidelity to human nature. Therefore, "*fidem rectumque*" is not a contradiction, but a complement. "*Fides*" is the passionate, patient, and passive aspect of human nature; "*rectum*" the dramatic, activist, active aspect through which nature is transformed into culture. The meadow is as it should be (in fact: intensified nature) for being the articulation of fidelity to nature. As our ancestors transformed the forest into meadow, they provoked and accentuated the natural essence in it. They continued to be faithful to it. The meadow, as culture (and not in spite of being culture), is essentially nature, because it was produced under the criterion of "*fides*;" under the criterion of an integrated religiosity.

Our ancestors were not landscape designers. They did not seek to integrate culture to nature. They did not feel the contradiction between culture and nature. They did not "*fidem rectumque colebant,*" that is, they did not synthesize faith with technology, and as they produced culture, they did not reveal the essence of nature. They were not – as landscape designers are – alienated from nature, or seeking to overcome this alienation through deliberate action. For them culture was what is natural to men, and therefore, appropriate to the whole of nature. And we, their alienated descendants, may still grasp some of their characteristic integration from the Golden Age as we lie in the meadow created by them so many thousands of years ago. The meadow allows us, as it allowed Ovid, to grasp also the meaning of the first verse of the epos: "*Aurea prima sata est aetas quae vindice nullo.*" (At the start, the Golden Age was sewn, and there were no judges.)

Winds

During some nights, the winds desperately howl around my house, because they cannot tear it down, or even enter it through a window or door left ajar. During these nights, my house is transformed into that fortified castle that resists the elements, as told in so many books of the past. Effectively, I feel sheltered and at peace with myself and with the world, while the winds seek to shake up the house's foundations. I know that the wind will come in, and that in this sense, it is different from thieves and the secret police. I have trust in the solidity of the house's construction (culture), in relation to the enormous, but blind, force of the elements of nature. Yet I do not have trust in its construction when one speaks of resisting smaller, more directed forces, such as the ones of culture. My house will not resist the police, thieves, or, even less, bombs. Not even an order from the City Council to demolish it. However, the difference between the wind and the police cannot be the same as the difference between blind forces and planned actions. For me, the winds, although blind, are predictable by meteorological forecast, but the police attack with surprise. That is because the winds obey a blind but publicly known order, which is therefore manageable. The police, thieves, and bombs obey partially secret, partially unknown, and partially contradictory orders, which are therefore unmanageable. The City Council, which obeys orders that apparently emanate from the public, apparently emits public orders, and apparently allows me to adapt myself to its orders and to influence them, is in reality a force against which all protection is ineffective. So that the force of the wind is quantifiable, but it is still not possible to say that the police attacked such a place at a certain time with a force of eight on whatever scale. The cultural sciences still have not reached, and perhaps never will, the same precision as the natural sciences. The bomb now provokes the terror once provoked by the hurricane. But the bomb's terror is profane. The sacred terror has now been overcome by the solidity of the house's construction.

However, one cannot deny that some of this lost sacredness still surrounds the wind. When they howl around my house I can still experience, although weakly (because I am protected by the house), the tremendous message that their howling once transmitted. And in the words of Jaroslav Vrchlický: "Jeho písen stala, veliky jest Alá" (In his constant song, great is Allah). This message is indebted maybe, to the fact that the wind is invisible. Even so, it is a thing, I know this perfectly well, because it can be measured, weighed, and pinpointed within space. But it is invisible, and this confuses our sense of "reality," which is a visual concept and not an auditory one. The wind confuses for example, the hierarchy imposed upon our minds by the syntax of our languages. This hierarchy is clear when it deals with visible things. In the sentence, "the Sun shines," there is no doubt that the "Sun" is the subject and "shines" the predicate. But the sentence, "the wind gusts" is reversible. "Gust" can be the subject and "wind" [*venta*] the predicate.[4] The wind is essentially an acoustic phenomenon (sound wave). The Sun, however, emits waves; it is the substantive of the waves. The wind is the verb itself, although substantiated. Strictly speaking, the wind cannot be predicated. To say that the wind gusts is tautological.

There are things in nature that are visible, but inaudible. The Sun, the Moon, the stars, in sum, the celestial things: "Substantive" things. Because they are inaudible, they are distant, and we cannot get closer. That is because vision is the sense that separates us from things, and hearing is the sense that submerges us in them. The seen world is circumstance; the world we hear, is a participated world. The things of nature that are audible but invisible, such as a hurricane and the breeze, penetrate through our noses, mouths and pores. They are "verbal," not "substantive." They are voices that call us. They run in the opposite direction than that of our own voices and can be incomparably more powerful (like the wind that howls around my house). However, they are essentially things of the same type. Since such things penetrate us, and as they are essentially like us, they are excessively close in order to be "contemplated." Therefore, they are not only invisible but also unimaginable. Our relation to

---

4 In Portuguese the noun *vento* (wind) may become the verb *ventar*, hence the possibility of the reversibility of the sentence. However, this is difficult to approximate in English. [TN]

such things is dialogic, and not imaginative. These are two limits of nature, two "sacred" aspects: the limit of visible but inaudible things, and the limit of audible but invisible things. The first is "substantial," and it is sacred because it is unapproachable. The second is "verbal," and it is sacred because it is unimaginable. The first may be called "spectral," if by "spectre" we understand a silent apparition. The second may be called "spiritual," if by "spirit" we understand an unimaginable breath.

Both of these "sacred" aspects are technically overcome, and in this sense humanity has surpassed the limits of nature. The Moon, one of the visible but inaudible things, was, as we say, "conquered." From goddess it became a platform. And the winds have, since long ago, propelled windmills and sails. From spirits that blow as they wish, they became forces that blow as we wish. And both "sacred" aspects are now theoretically overcome, through a profaning synthesis. The "wind" becomes "energy," the "Sun" becomes "matter," and one becomes, theoretically, a reversible aspect of the other. Formally speaking, we have thus invented mathematical language, in which there are no longer substantives and verbs, but only relational functions – and these functions function, for example, in the form of the bomb. Through a theoretical synthesis that works in practice we have profaned both "sacred" aspects, the "spectres" became "spirits" and the "spirits" became "spectres," and our terror is from now on profane. This is the terror of the equations, and it is under the "equilibrium of terror" that we live today.

Both of these "sacred" aspects are technically and theoretically overcome, but not existentially. During some nights, when the wind desperately howls around my house, I can still hear the "sacred" voice, despite the solidity of the house's construction, despite the theoretical information at my disposal. Both the solidity and the information at my disposal definitely interfere with the wind's message, but they cannot destroy it. They interfere in the following manner: my mind is the product of two contradictory traditions that have never been satisfactorily synthetized: the tradition of the voice and the tradition of the image. That of the commandment, and that of the idea. That of the verb, and that of the substantive. That of the existential decision, and that of speculative metaphysics. I cannot simplify the dilemma by saying that the tradition of the invisible is Jewish and that that of the inaudible is Greek. This dilemma is anterior to both of my mind's foundational cultures. In Jewish culture there already were imaginative elements, although the prophets tried hard to expurgate them. And in Greek culture there already were dialogic elements, even though the "logos" always tends toward idealization. The dilemma between "wind" and "celestial thing" is not the one between "*olam habá*" and "*topos uranikós*" (the world to come and the celestial place), but is the much older dilemma between the "being-in-the-world" of he who hears and he who sees, of he who is called and makes up his mind, and of he who removes the veil and contemplates. Such a dilemma is impossible to overcome, because to subscribe to only one of the alternatives is to amputate half of one's own mind. And this interferes with the reception of the message from the wind that howls around my house.

But the wind cannot destroy it. Because the wind howls; that is, it speaks. Therefore, the wind is not a thing. Things do not speak. The wind is not a something; it is a someone to whom I must respond, it is a You that calls me in order to be an I. Because it is a You, the wind cannot be imagined, conceived, known or manipulated. It must be heard, received, recognized, and followed. When the wind is imagined, conceived, known, and manipulated, as it is technically and theoretically, it stops being the wind and becomes the movement of the air; it becomes "objectified." But the wind is not an object: it is my Other. It is not a being; it exists. That is why Buber says: "God is not: I believe in Him." And Angelus Silesius: "*Ich weiss ohne mich Gott nicht ein Nu kann leben.*" (I know that without me God cannot live an instant.) The wind is the wind for me, if I allow it to be the wind. And if I do not allow it, it will be the movement of the air and not the wind. If I do not allow it to be the wind, it will be a partially resolved problem of aerodynamics. But if I allow it to be the wind, it will be an enigma. If I do not allow it to be the wind, it will lose its voice; it will become air vibrations, to be manipulated in decibels. It will become mute. But now, tonight, when it desperately howls around my house, the wind speaks, because I am prepared to listen to it. That is why the prayer that says "*Chema Israel, JHVH elohenu JHVH ekhád*" (listen, God's fighter, JHVH is our God, JHVH is one) is a prayer, and not an indicative statement. It says: "listen!" The wind that desperately howls around my house indicates nothing; it is imperious. If I allow it that, then that is its message. Despite all the interferences I still receive this message during nights like this one.

These interferences certainly make it so that I no longer receive the message in an "orthodox" way. Neither Jews, Christians, nor Muslims (those who state that they are receiving the message in an "orthodox" way) will be able to affirm the message that I am receiving is the "true" one. They will state that the voice of the wind that surrounds my house is not the true voice, and that I am being superstitious in allowing the wind to speak. But the dialogue with these orthodoxies is difficult for me. I am unable to hear the voices that they say they hear (the "true" ones), and I must admit that I am suspicious, not so much of the fact that they are heard, but more of the veracity of these voices. That is because I doubt that it is possible to eliminate the technical and theoretical interferences up to the point of allowing the voices to speak. I suspect that orthodoxies violate these interferences in order to hear, and that, as a consequence, what they hear is false. But I do not insist too much on my distrust, doubt, and suspicion. I am prepared to hypothetically admit, with a slight hint of jealousy, that they may hear what I do not hear. As for myself, I must be satisfied with the enigma that I hear from the wind that howls around my house. Who knows: maybe this enigma is the same for them as it is for me? An enigma that must, but cannot be, deciphered?

The wind howls around my house tonight. I feel sheltered, because I know that contrary to the nefarious forces of culture, the wind cannot enter my house. And I simultaneously seek to allow, in spite of this, the wind to speak to me; to penetrate me, without penetrating me.

This is the dialectic between the knowledge that closes itself as it objectifies, and the recognition that opens itself as it allows the Other to be. This situation is unbearable, because it mines both knowledge and recognition. This is the characteristic situation of the end of a game, or of the start of a new one. It is the loss of knowledge in faith and of faith in knowledge. In the situation in which the visible becomes invisible, and the audible inaudible. This is our situation, despite so much talk of "audiovisuality." It is necessary for the wind to howl furiously, in order for me to hear it a little and only barely. But I know that the wind that surrounds my house is, objectively speaking, the movement of a gas, and I know, objectively speaking, that the word "gas" has the same etymological root as the word "chaos." So that I know that what surrounds my house has no grounding, even though it is meteorologically predictable and even though it obeys blind rules. This knowledge of mine, of the groundlessness under the laws that rule nature, is a knowledge that is almost recognition. It is a way of losing one's faith in knowledge, through knowledge. It is not, certainly, a conquest of "faith," in the sense that the orthodoxies give to the term. But it is still a type of openness all the same. Because the "chaos" of which the wind speaks to me is not a case of Brownian motion of gas around my house. It is the howling "chaos." And this is my interpretation of the message from the howling: "and this is all the wisdom I can reap: I came like water, and like wind I go."[5]

---

[5] This last sentence, which is rendered in English in the original, is also a reference to the *Rubaiyat* of Omar Khayyam (1048-1123). [TN]

Wonders

I know that one of the traditional "proofs" of the existence of God is that nature reveals a specific purpose, that is, a creative deliberation. I cannot remember the first time I was exposed to this argument, but I do not doubt that it must have occurred during a walk, and that it must have been my nanny who initiated my tender young mind to metaphysics and theology by pointing to a wonderful flower or the wonderful color of a bird. It must have been my nanny and not my mother, because nannies tend more toward Romanticism than mothers. I cannot even remember how many times and under which varied forms the same argument in favor of a God, creator of the world, was repeated to me. It must have been several times, and under ever more complex forms. But I do remember, very clearly, the first time when I experienced the falsity of this "proof." I must have been around eight years old, and my uncle had taken me fishing. He showed me how to hook the earthworms and the experience of the earthworm in my hand made it so that the ideology of a God, creator of a wonderful world, evaporated completely. It must have been a strong experience, a mixture of disgust, pity, and a feeling of guilt, but what must have prevailed was the discovery of the brutal stupidity of a supposed creator of earthworms, fishes, and fishermen. It is difficult to retrospectively analyze what happened then in my young mind, but I do remember perfectly well that I stopped believing in a creator-God out of pity for God, as if I had intuitively understood the hypothesis that a creator-God is contrary to any faith in a God of love and hope. Intuitively, I must have understood that the God who was responsible for the earthworm's death was not the God I prayed to every night "for all adults and children." It is obvious that I am falsifying my childhood experience by saying that "I opted against the philosophers' God in order to preserve the existential God," but these are the words that come to me in the attempt to explain what I experienced then.

I do not know how typical this sort of experience is, but it must be very typical, since at eight years old there cannot be much originality. So if it is typical for an eight year-old to refuse the "proof" of the existence of God through the observation of nature, then several questions arise. These questions may be ordered into three groups: a) sociological questions, b) theological questions, and c) epistemological questions. The sociological ones ask how, why, and when the hypothesis of a creator-God emerged, how it managed to resist the critiques of those older than eight years of age, and how such critiques could be formulated despite the formidable pressure exerted by this ideology upon eight year-olds. The theological questions ask how faith manages to resist the dead weight of the dogma of a creator-God, how such dogma can be absorbed by a "dialogic" religiosity, and why should it be maintained despite all the insurmountable moral, scientific, and philosophical difficulties. However, it is the epistemological questions that are interesting at this moment, as I sit on my sunny terrace contemplating the wonders of nature. This is because it was the contemplation of such wonders that motivated the memory of the "proof" of God as the creator of nature.

The scene I am contemplating (a wintery landscape, reluctantly awakening under the precipitating rays of an almost spring-like sun) is covered by several of my culture's "explanatory" and "interpretative" layers: by my prejudices. To contemplate it means exactly to seek to remove, or pierce, or to turn transparent such covering layers, with the aim of seeing the landscape immediately. A desperate task, because cultural mediations that interpose themselves between myself and the scene are my way of being in the scene. Immediate communication, the *"unio mystica,"* sought through contemplation, is a desperate aim, for it is a prejudice imposed by my culture. There are methods, techniques, exercises, Yogas, "phenomenological reductions," etc., which affirm to be able to provoke such immediate communication, however, such technical approaches are themselves a good reason for us to be suspicious. Because it seems to be contradictory to wish to reach an immediate contact mediated by something: to wish to deliberate about spontaneity. There is an empirical and pragmatic flavor to mysticism that turns it sour. Nevertheless, to contemplate, in the sense of seeking to let go of explanations and interpretations, is not necessarily a failed endeavor: although it may not lead to an unmediated communication with that which is contemplated, it may remove prejudices. Contemplation may be critical and not discursive of explanatory and interpretative discourses.

The layers that cover-up the scene that I am contemplating are projections of my mind, which, in its turn, is a system that has been programmed by my culture's history. Effectively, an efficient method in order for me to become aware of my programming is to critique the layers that cover-up the scene. I recognize myself in the covering layers, furthermore: *I am* these layers; *I am* this specific covering-up of the scene. In seeking to remove this layer, I am effectively trying to remove myself from the scene, in order to allow the scene to be itself. And in seeking to remove myself, I verify what I am: a system that has been historically programmed in order to capture the scene. This is the first step of contemplation: to verify that the observation of nature is a critique of history and culture.

I can clearly distinguish the three famous types within the covering layers: the aesthetic ones, the ethical ones and the explanatory ones. Thanks to the first type I am experiencing the contemplated scene hyper-realistically, expressionistically, impressionistically, naturally, romantically, and so on. My concrete experience of the contemplated scene "repeats the phylogenesis of art." Not "correctly," for sure. I commit anachronisms. And I am not operating within my own time. At the moment, for example, I am experiencing the scene "classically," and this is the first reason for my sense of wonder: why is it that the contemplated scene "is so similar" to the scenes of the seventeen hundreds?

Thanks to the ethical layers, I am being provoked by the scene in order to engage myself in it, or against it. It is not so easy to discover the stratification of these layers, as in the case of the aesthetic ones, maybe because the history of "practical reason" is contradictory and full of fallbacks. But I can, definitely, distinguish three basic forms, three "behavioral models." The contemplated scene is not as it ought to be, so I must change it. The contemplated scene either invites me to let go of myself within it, or it is nothing more than the backdrop of the stage on which I act. Without a doubt, the fact that I remembered the earthworm indicates that I am, at this moment, taking on the first behavioral model. I find the scene that I see, revolting and cruel, I shake with justifiable anger, and I would like to "remold it nearer to the heart's desire."[6] But I know, simultaneously, that such a revolutionary attitude is part of my program. And this is the second reason for my sense of wonder: why is it that today the scene calls me to battle, whereas yesterday the same scene called me to delight passively in peace?

My memory of the earthworms provokes, above all, a critique of the explanatory layers during the contemplation of the scene. The fact is, although these layers seem to mutually overcome each other, they do not cancel each other out. And this is the third and greatest reason for my sense of wonder. Without a doubt, the explanatory layers are "progressive," and the most recent

---

6 Idem.

gives a "better" explanation than the older ones. "Better," because it dialectically synthesizes the older ones. In this respect the explanatory layers distinguish themselves structurally from the other two types. It does not make sense to say that the hyper-realistic layer allows for a "better" experience of the scene than the classicist layer, or that the revolutionary model of behavior allows me to act "better" within the scene than the neutralizing model. But it does make sense to say that the explanation of the origin of life that I contemplate in the scene, offered by Jacques Monod, is "better" than the one offered by the thesis that "God is the creator of life." However, if that is how it is, why is it that the overcome layers do not disappear? Why do they continue to cover-up the scene? This is, effectively, the question that was provoked by the memory of the earthworm: why is it that even though I now know how to explain the life around me much better, the explanation "God" continues to confuse my view of the scene?

I believe that I have the answer to the question, but I do not like it. The origin of life given by Jacques Monod is obviously "formal": a game. Monod speaks of the "game of the evolution of the RNA" and points to its three rules: steric, complementariness, and cooperativeness. Given such rules, life becomes explainable as a "necessary" process, in the curious sense of chance being a necessity. And not only does it become explainable, but also, theoretically, reconstructible. Whoever knows the game may create life and enable it to evolve. Theoretically. Thus, this is what characterizes the explanatory layers. The most recent are more formal, more of the type "game," than the previous ones, and therefore "better." The previous ones are "worse" because to say that God created life does not explain anything, it does not indicate the rules of the game. And that is why the previous layers cannot be removed. They cover-up the scene better because they do not indicate rules. They work better as covering layers because they do not work "well." And they make the scene more visible because they cover it up better. Within Monod's type of explanation, the scene becomes almost invisible: I no longer see life, only the empty game. In order to see, I need heavy mediation, for example, God. If I "refine" God, I no longer see the scene.

I do not like this one bit. So I need God as the creator of the world in order to see the world, even though I know that God is a terrible explanation for the world? Even though I know that if I accept this creator-God I cannot love Him? So I need God to prevent the world from evaporating into empty and transparent forms, even though I know that the "non-evaporated" world is an apparent context made up of earthworms on hooks? And more: not only do I need but I also demand such a God, how can I not get rid of Him? I do not like this, and this not liking of mine is the wonder of wonders. The world is wonderful because if I "discover" it, it disappears, and if I leave it covered it becomes horrible. And finally, because both alternatives are not real options: I am obligated to both. To "formalism" as well as to the "worm-like feeling." I am obligated to "refine God," as well as to believe in the Creator despite all of the progressive explanations at my disposal.

I know perfectly well that nature, if analyzed, will not reveal a Divine purpose but a blind game between chance and necessity. And I feel that if I decide to see a purpose in nature, it would be diabolic and not Divine. And simultaneously, I know that if I get rid of the Demiurge (something I cannot do), nature will disappear in front of my eyes. All of this epistemological, ethical, and aesthetic confusion is my way of facing nature and seeking to overcome the abyss that separates me from it. Is this not wonderful? Yes, nature is wonderful: it consists of earthworms on hooks in which I admire a Creator that I know is nothing more than a projection of a cretinous dialectic between chance and necessity.

Buds

The branches of the apple tree under my terrace have changed since yesterday. When I saw them last they looked like elements of an empty structure, and they were, as it is fitting to structural elements, gray, bare and light. Yesterday, the orchard that surrounds my house effectively offered a "structural" and "formal" vision in the radical sense of such terms. The context was composed of structures of the "tree" type; that is, it was composed of ramified forms. These "trees" were certainly complex structures. Not only did the branches spring from the trunk at geometrically determinable places, to then bifurcate several times hierarchically, but there was also a disturbing element to this order. The branches contorted, seemingly crossing each other at several places, and some of the branches were stronger than others. But this did not stop them to serve as structural models. On the contrary, for being complex structures, they were better to be filled by content. My vision of the apple trees projected several types of content upon them. For example: this tree here "illustrated" the structure of the evolution of life, this other the structure of the genealogy of fusional languages, and this third one the structure of the natural sciences. This branch here "represented" the branch of the vertebrates, and this other here the branch of the Latin languages, and this third one the branch of inorganic chemistry. And the vision of my orchard allowed, yesterday, for a very entertaining game of fantasy. This apple tree would not have been good for Darwin because its branches tended to form a horizontal treetop, but it served perfectly well for the genealogy of the Habsburgs. And this other apple tree was more useful for the genealogy of languages, because several branches crisscrossed to then separate, and because its trunk was composed of several sub-trunks.

This game of fantasy is no longer possible. This is because it rained during the night, and today, when I opened the window, I saw that the branches of the apple trees had changed. They are covered in buds, which I know (although I cannot see them) will be pinkish-white flowers. For now they are modest buds, slight disturbances barely visible on the smooth surface of the branches. A kind of apple tree skin disease; however, I know that this illness is a symptom of health. During the night the apple trees awoke to their destiny. The "virtual" in them (the flower) erupted: it came to the surface. "Necessity" was added to the "virtual" overnight and came, this morning, to be "reality." The miracle of transfiguration acted upon the apple trees overnight. The ontological leap from the merely possible to the effectively real happened. The future transformed into present. Yesterday, the flower was within the future of the apple tree; today it is present. For the apple trees the trumpets sounded during the night: they are all changed. This ontological revolution no longer allows me to see them as if they were structures. I am obliged, therefore, to see them as if they were tendencies toward a destiny. Tendencies toward the flower and the fruit. Not that their structural aspect has been eliminated, but that it has been "*aufgehoben.*" The structures now support a process, a process that seeks a specific aim. Apples, and not the Habsburgs or the genealogy of languages, are now the "content" of the form of the apple trees. This miracle (because every ontological leap, every revolution, is a miracle) is called "spring." And it does not matter that it repeats itself every year. In the "*kyklos tes geneseos*" it does not matter that it is a cycle. What matters is that it is about generation, the emergence of something new. The generative form, the revolutionary process, superimposes itself over the cyclical form, the repetitive form, and this is the miracle. The eternal return as the will to power, the buds of every March as a revolution, Nietzsche and Marx as twin brothers: that is how I am obliged to "read" my apple trees.

What I see, therefore, as I look at my orchard, is no longer a structural, but a tragic view: I see destiny. That is why I said that I am obliged to "read" the apple trees. It is written on them ("*maktub*") that they will bear fruit. Thus they shall be; they shall not be able to escape it. ("*So must du sein, dir kannst du nicht entfliehen*").[7] I no longer see structures: I see Oedipus in my orchard. I comprehend, as I look at the buds, why Oedipus, tragically seeking to escape his destiny, in reality fulfilled it. To kill his father, sleep with his mother, and pull out his eyes is as fateful for Oedipus as it is for the apple trees to irrupt with

---

7   Goethe, J. *Urworte. Orphisch*, 1817.

buds, blossom with flowers, bear fruit, lose their leaves, and crystalize into a structure. For Oedipus, to wish to avoid killing his father is, for the apple tree, to wish not to bloom. If he had not killed his father, he would not have been Oedipus, and if they had not irrupted with buds, they would not have been apple trees. However, there is one difference between Oedipus and my apple trees: hubris, a condemnable and condemned heroism that is impossible for the apple trees. They are tragic without even knowing it. They are unconscious Oedipuses. Their tragedy exists for me, not for themselves. But who knows, maybe Schopenhauer was right, and tragedy is a common ocean from which apple trees and I sprung during this spring: a tragic will that is represented by both the apple trees on one side, and myself on the other?

But how is all of this possible? How can the buds impose such a tragic vision of the world upon me? The very term "destiny" sounds very strange to my ears. It does not fit in any way to my experience of time. I do not think "finalistically," but "causally" or "structurally." The world is not a tragedy for me, but a theatre of the absurd. For me, the future is not a fatalistically "predetermined" aim, but an open horizon of realizable virtualities. For me, the way is not a journey in search of a destination ("destiny"), but an aimless adventurous journey ("sense"). For me, "futuration" is not to discover the end ("finality"), but the prospection of what is possible ("freedom"). For me, to live is not to find sense, but to give sense. The tragic feeling of the world (fatalism) is not strange to me, but it is a submersed feeling. What dominates for me is the experience of the absurd. For me, "necessity" is not the end, but the cause. For me, nature is not a book that I must read in order to live "correctly." I am neither Orphic nor Mohammedian. For me, nature is a meaningless set of elements that acquires meaning only when my peers and I transform it into culture. For me, this is what distinguishes nature from culture: culture is a readable text (a codified world) written upon a meaningless natural backdrop ("*wertfrei* = exempt of values"). How can the buds revolve, therefore, around the categories imposed upon me by my anti-tragic and anti-fatalist culture?

The question may easily be averted if I resort to formal logic, but not even then will it be resolved. Formally, I may say that there are three types of "explanations": (a) the finalistic ones that say "for," (b) the causal ones that say "because of," and (c) the structural ones that say "in this form." For example: (a) birds build nests *for* keeping their eggs, (b) birds build nests *because of* their instincts, and (c) birds build nests *in the form* of cones. The (a) type of explanation is more satisfactory because it turns what is explained into something that makes sense. The (c) type of explanation is less satisfactory because it only explains structurally. The history of thought starts with explanations of the (a) type, then sees itself obliged to abandon them in favor of explanations of the (b) type, and currently it is also painstakingly abandoning causality in favor of formalism. The history of thought is, therefore, the history of explanations that become less satisfactory along the course of time. But this erosion of satisfaction (and of meaning) does not happen within all fields with the same rhythm. To say that, "it rains in order to wet the earth" is currently an unacceptable explanation.

But to say that, "animals have eyes to see" is less offensive. Effectively, biology is less formal than physics, because finalistic explanations are less offensive to the phenomena it deals with. The buds impose a tragic feeling of the world upon me because they are biological phenomena, which finalistic explanations do not offend so much. But I can easily get rid of this tragic feeling if I remember that currently there already are causal and formal explanations for buds, which makes this tragic feeling anachronic, primitive, and "overcome."

The question has been thus averted, but by no means resolved, because the answer introduced the concept of "satisfaction" without having elaborated it. "Satisfaction" is precisely what this is about. When I look at the buds that irrupt on my apple trees, causal and formal explanations do not satisfy me. And satisfaction is the only existential criterion of truth. It is what Heidegger calls "*das stimmt*" = thus it is correct. A "Stimmung" = a climate of buds and of spring in the tragic sense of the world. So, finalistic "explanations" and the future as a destiny are "true" in this case. To explain buds and spring causally or structurally is to "explain them away," it is to de-explain them. And the question is precisely this: why do buds and spring impose such a tragic feeling upon me, and evoke the future as a destiny, despite all other explanations, which therefore, become unsatisfactory and explain nothing?

I am neither Orphic nor Mohammedian, and nature is for me neither a collection of symbols nor a book written by Allah. I do not believe that it is possible to "decipher" nature in order to discover thus its "deep meaning," nor do I believe that Allah, in his love for humanity, dictated to his prophet a second book, the *Al Quran*, which allows for the reading of the first book, that of nature. I am convinced that nature is a set of meaningless and purposeless elements and that the search for human dignity entails giving meaning to nature by imposing human purposes upon it. Effectively, I am convinced that to humanize nature is to realize it, and that, if not humanized, nature is nothing more than a mere human virtuality. For example: I am convinced that the buds that I am contemplating have nothing tragic in them, but seek to turn into apples, which will be transformed into juice, for which Meran is famous. The apple trees are there because horticulturists planted them. They are not part of nature, but of culture. They have purpose and meaning: purpose and meaning that were imposed upon them by the horticulturists; however, the buds in my orchard still speak their own unsophisticated language. They speak of transfiguration, tragic, and trans-human purpose, and they speak of destiny. And what they say is true. Although they are culture, they continue to be nature in this miraculous and mysterious meaning of the term.

Therefore I cannot give an answer to the question. I am a victim of two honesties or dishonesties. It is dishonest to deny that my orchard obeys human purposes, that it is a realization of the beautiful human will that imposes itself upon a mere natural virtuality, and thus endows it with value and meaning. And it is dishonest to deny that my orchard gives a meaning to the horticulturalists' lives, a meaning that they "chose" themselves (however problematically). But it is equally dishonest to deny that the buds which irrupted last night articulate fundamental forces, and that the juices which pulsate in apple tree branches also tragically pulsate within my veins and propels, both the apple trees and me, toward an inescapable destiny. I cannot give an answer to the question, except perhaps this: the "Oedipal hubris," the tragic heroism that is human dignity, is to make orchards and apple juice as a desperate challenge to the tragic and mysterious juice that irrupts at certain catastrophic moments such as in the buds of spring.

Fog

For several days now the weather report has started its broadcast with the same sentence: "after the persistent morning fog has lifted...." And, effectively, every morning these days I wake up with that milky white light of a Sun that cannot break through the veils that cover it. Unfortunately this is a situation that is so laden with literature and clichés that I have great difficulty experiencing it concretely. The morning fog is "covered by a thick ideological fog" that needs to be removed in order for me to see the non-metaphorical fog out there. This removal effort will show that it is possible to divide humanity into two types: those who like and those who do not like diffused light. The "fans" of unsolved mysteries and the ones that solve crossword puzzles. The profound ones and the enlightened ones. The inspired ones and the suspicious ones. The ones who are interested in the general and universal depths from which all things are vaguely distinguished, and the ones who are interested in the differences through which all things distinguish themselves from one another. In sum, the metaphysicians and the phenomenologists. The first type seeks to penetrate the fog, and the second type seeks to remove it. Because the first affirms and the second negates. They are, I believe, two fundamentally opposed attitudes and in between them rises the great water barrier that divides humanity. But they are different attitudes, not situations. All men, for being men, are in the fog, whether they like it or not.

Well, I do not want to be in the fog. However, I have to confess that the attitude of the fog's "fans" is not strange to me, and that although I repeatedly fall victim of the seduction exerted by "mystery," I have opted for the attitude of suspicion. To remove the fog and to try to show that it is fog and not something else seems to me to be a dignified attitude. I opted against profundity in favor of superficiality. This is because I believe that nothing profound hides behind the fog, and that the fog is an illusion that covers up a concrete surface, behind which nothing hides. This is not, even though it seems so, a game with words. Contrary to the profound thinkers, I do not believe that the ultimate aim is to reach the deepest part of the fog, but that after it has been uncovered, then the real task begins: to try to apprehend and comprehend the exposed surface. Deep thought seems to me to be more superficial than the thought that seeks to grasp the surface of things. I believe that the German profundity of the first half of the twentieth century is more superficial than the Anglo-Saxon superficiality of the same period. I am with Goethe when he says: "*Man suche nur nichts hinter den Phänomenen. Sie selbst sind die Lehre.*" (Let us not search for anything behind phenomena. They are themselves the teachings.) That is why I shall try to remove the metaphorical fog that covers the morning fog, in order to try to see it concretely.

I live in a house from whose terrace a vast panorama unfolds. A wide valley surrounded by several rows of ice-covered peaks. The view goes from the nearest mountains all the way to the majestic summits on the horizon. But not today. Today I see only the orchard that surrounds my house, and I can guess, just vaguely, the outlines of the pine trees that surround my orchard. Today my horizon is narrow. But as I say this, two doubts jump at me. The first says that had I not seen the panorama yesterday, today I would not know that my horizon is narrow. The second says that every horizon is equally wide because they are horizons; that is, the limits of the finite toward to the infinite. The first doubt implies that the fog is a limitation only for those who know that it is a fog. The second implies that to wish to widen horizons by removing fog is an absurd effort. Both doubts must be considered under the prism of the concrete fog that surrounds my house, and the second before the first.

There is an anecdote that tells of the conquest of Syracuse by the Romans. A centurion entered Archimedes' house in order to invite him to be the engineer of the Roman legions. Archimedes declined the offer, affirming that he did not have enough time for that. He was too absorbed with the problems of the circle. The centurion was amazed at such alienation: how could one be worried about circles, when the Roman Empire was conquering the *Orbis terrarum*? "Exactly," said Archimedes, "I intend to show that it is of no use to enlarge the circumference of circles because the relation between the circumference and the radius is constant." In the face of such subversive alienation the centurion had no choice but to kill Archimedes. The anecdote cannot be archived as a parable of the conflict between engaging with history or engaging with forms, because the real problem, shown by the anecdote, is this: if formally seen, progress has no aim, and if to widen horizons is to remain in the same form, then what is the sense in studying forms? In other words, if the Archimedean circles made Roman war machines absurd (even though they were based on the circles), then what was Archimedes doing? Pure theory? An overcoming of politics through the contemplation of pure forms? Yes, but as he contemplated forms, was Archimedes also not widening horizons? That is, was he stuck on the same form? The problem of the anecdote is this: the Archimedean argument against the centurion may be turned against Archimedes himself. Not like this: the centurion is a progressive and Archimedes an alienated reactionary. But like this: Archimedes is as progressive, and therefore absurd, as the centurion. They both advance by dissolving the fog. But this is a different fog. If the Archimedean argument is correct, theory is as absurd as praxis, and so in Syracuse and today, what remains is only cynicism and stoicism.

The cynical position in relation to the fog that surrounds my house is this: the horizon that I see today is as good as the one I saw yesterday. The Brazilian *caboclo*'s horizon is as good as that of a Harvard student. And the stoic position in relation to the fog that surrounds my house is this: if I accept today's horizon as I accepted yesterday's, I shall be content with both. The *caboclo* will be happy, not if he seeks to widen his horizon, but if he seeks to be content with it. The cynical and stoic positions are as logically and existentially insurmountable today as they were in Syracuse, and in this sense, the Archimedean argument against the centurion and against Archimedes is still perfect. Both positions are the true overcoming of politics, not through theory, but through the negation of values. But they are ethically unbearable positions today as well as in Syracuse, and the fog that surrounds my house is proof of that. I only need to leave the terrace and walk toward the pine trees that line the horizon. The horizon will recede according to my steps. Yesterday, when there was no fog, the horizon would not have receded. The nebulous horizon is ethically (practically) removable because it recedes. The horizon of a clear vision does not recede. They are two different horizons. The first is an undignified condition; it limits me because I allow it. The second is a dignified condition, because I cannot go beyond it. That is why I must engage in clear horizons and against nebulous ones. Because it is only after I have removed the nebulous horizons that I will be able to see the real limits that are imposed upon me. To want to remove the fog is not, therefore, an ethically absurd effort, because it does not seek "to widen horizons" (yes, that would be absurd), but to find the real horizons to be those that cannot be widened. "To de-ideologize" is not to set-free (yes, that would be absurd), but to allow the real conditions to emerge.

    The other doubt provoked by my fog, the one that says the fog is only so for those who already know that it is a fog, cannot be pragmatically disproved as the one already considered, because it affirms that he who does not live in my house, but knows of yesterday's panorama, has no reason to walk toward the pine trees. He is, one could say, a spontaneous cynic and stoic, not a deliberate one. He accepts the limitation of the fog, and is content to adapt himself because he takes it to be real. This doubt effectively affirms that he who is a victim of ideology cannot be aware of it, because he takes his ideology to be objective knowledge. This is the well-known Marxist theory. That is why, according to Marxism, any ideology can only be removed by the oppressing class (the only ones that are aware of ideologies). "The bourgeoisie is the proletariat's conscience." And that is why the oppressed resist the efforts to remove ideologies: they are spontaneous cynics and stoics. Example: Che Guevara and the Bolivian peasants. Therefore, within the oppressing class itself, there is no contradiction (the dialectic conscience of ideology), so there would never be a need to remove ideologies. All the "opiates" would work eternally, because they would work perfectly.

But the concrete fog that surrounds my house allows for the dissipation of this doubt in the following manner: although the concrete fog and the metaphorical one are similar phenomena (both cover up reality), the concrete fog is a natural phenomenon and the metaphorical one a cultural phenomenon. The concrete one is given and the metaphorical one made-up. The concrete one is a covering of reality by reality itself; the metaphorical one is a deliberate covering of reality by producers of veils ("*Schleiermacher*"). Therefore we must make the distinction between two types of "mysteries": the obscurity of reality itself, and the obscurity made-up by obscurantists. In other words, even if we managed to remove all of the ideological fogs, we would still not find reality's resplendent surface, but concrete fogs as the one surrounding my house. The indignity of the ideologues is not, therefore, of obscuring the clarity of reality, but the mystery of reality. The primitive and naive Marxists (not the authentic and sophisticated ones) commit an error in believing that to remove ideology means to achieve a de-alienation from reality. Such a belief is in itself an ideology. To remove ideologies is, on the contrary, to open oneself up to concrete fogs. It is in this sense that Ernst Bloch can say that real religiosity will only be possible after the dissolution of established religions. This is essentially his "principle of hope."

The concrete fog that surrounds my house is not only for whoever saw the panorama yesterday. It emanates a different climate. The climate yesterday was one of clarity, in which differences appeared. Today's is of a diffuse light, in which differences are blurred. Yesterday it was "natural" to distinguish and today it is "natural" to dive into the indistinct. Yesterday it was reason and today it is intuition that is "adequate" to the scene. Even though I do not want to be in the fog, even though I prefer yesterday's panorama, I cannot avoid today's climate. Even though I want to belong with the suspicious crowd, I cannot stop from inhaling the concrete nebulosity that surrounds me. Precisely for having tried to remove the metaphorical fog, I am obliged to allow the concrete fog to bathe and penetrate me through my pores. And this is the "phenomenon's teaching" (to converse with Goethe):

religious feeling concretely imposes itself only after the attempt to deny and remove the ideological veils of established religions.

I do not know if there is any sense in talking about "natural religiosity" provoked by climates such as the one of the fog that surrounds my house. Perhaps it would be better to talk of "transcultural religiosity," or religiosity after the disillusionment with made-up religions. The fog that surrounds my house is not, autobiographically speaking, anterior to the ideological fogs that obscure my view of things. It is posterior to them, and visible after a deliberate effort to remove them. The authentic "*Homo religiosus*" is not "primitive." The "primitive" (if he exists) is a victim of even more grotesque ideologies. The authentic "*Homo religiosus*" is suspicious (disillusioned). He is the one who discovered that the removal of metaphorical fogs results in a dive into concrete fogs. Who knows, maybe dignity is this: to remove metaphorical fogs in order to dive into concrete ones? To be anti-obscurantist in order to dive into the real darkness? But here, the terrible difficulty of distinguishing between given and made-up obscurity must be confessed. But we must make a distinction between them. It is only thanks to distinction (reason) that we can dive into the real fog.

Natural:Mind
(a kind of conclusion)

The essays in this book do not demand, if considered individually, an introduction. They can stand alone, each one, under their own weight. And when they do not, they fail as essays. Considered one by one, the essays do not form a whole. Read as such, they may be read in any sequence: they are as disparate as their themes. Seen through this prism, the present book is a bundle of essays, in the sense of having been harvested without a criterion for choice. That is: an occasional collection, the fruit of chance. The subjects that the essays deal with occurred to the author along the course of his life, and were dealt with as they happened: casually. Those who have acquired the habit of allowing every occasional subject to occupy the center of their attention, and those who take it as a pretext in order to let go of a flux of reflections, know the fascination exerted by any type of encounter with any type of experience (which then becomes an adventure). They know, therefore, the motive for the present book. This also explains, organically, the stylistic differences between the essays. Each essay has its style imposed upon it by its subject. But the dialectic "subject/style," or "content/form," problematizes this statement. Certainly, the subject imposes itself upon the style. Equally certain, is that every subject is a subject only after it has been taken on in one form or another. The stylistic difference of the present essays is, therefore, a consequence of the dialectic game through which several occasional experiences imposed themselves upon the author, and that were taken on by him in order to become subjects for essays. Hence, neither the subjects nor the style of the present essays demand an introductory explanation. They are occasional; the fruit of the chances in living, and chance cannot and does not need to be explained. It happens "naturally."

However, the present book also allows itself to be read on another level. And since this level, although implicit in the essays, is not explained within them, the author finds himself obliged to write an explanatory conclusion. Here it is. Being fascinated by the inexhaustible richness of concrete experiences, and by the catalyzing power that every experience has upon thought, the author wrote, along the course of the last several years, a whole series of essays like the ones in this volume. Those essays were, in large part, published in several Brazilian, American, German and French periodicals, and especially in the *Suplemento Literário* of the *Estado de São Paulo* newspaper. In retrospect, what impressed the author was the fact that the subjects of all the essays are experiences with cultural things. It is as if all the experiences, which the author went through during these recent years, had exclusively been encounters with the culture that surrounds us. Almost as if nature had not existed for him, or as if it had been pushed toward the horizon of his everyday experience. Two interpretations of this fact emerged: (a) the author is an "intellectual" and has lost contact with nature, and (b) technological and administered society, in which the author participates, has lost such a contact. Both interpretations are probably correct, but they do not satisfy. There must be a more radical and less obvious reason that the author and society no longer experience nature, or that they do it, but only exceptionally. And this reason must be linked to a mutation of the concept, of the experience, and of the value meant by "nature." A mutation that is currently underway.

In order to find such a reason, or at least, in order to come closer to it, the author did two things: (a) I collected ten already published essays and published them in Paris under the title *La Force du Quotidien*. The chosen essays deal with the experiences of indubitably cultural things, with instruments, such as: walking sticks, bottles, pens, eyeglasses, rugs, walls, mirrors, books, beds and cars. The aim of the selection was to illustrate the power exerted by instruments (by culture) upon everyday life, to illustrate how culture, far from freeing man from the determining forces of nature, constitutes itself as a determining condition. Therefore, as a "second nature." Thus, the author sought to illustrate how today's man experiences culture: not as something made, but as something given, therefore, as nature. Today's man has lost touch with the nature of the traditional meaning of the term (or is losing it) because culture is taking on the existential impact of nature in the traditional meaning of the term. (b) Not satisfied with such a "negative proof," the author sought to open himself up, deliberately at the beginning, then always more spontaneously, to experiences meant as natural in the traditional meaning of the term. The results are the present essays. The initial motivation was the suspicion that the existential impact of natural experiences are indistinguishable from cultural ones, and that, therefore, the ontological distinction between nature and culture is not existentially sustainable within the current context. According to this suspicion, the ontological distinction to be made today would be between determining-experiences and freeing-experiences, two ontological categories that ignore the traditional categories of "nature/culture" or "given/made." Now, as he reconsiders the essays presented here, the author is incapable of saying whether the initial suspicion was confirmed or refuted by his research.

This is not, in the author's opinion, necessarily a defect. An "essay" is this: the attempt to see where a working hypothesis ends up. And the interesting thing about the essay is not the result, the confirmed or refuted hypothesis. The interesting thing is what emerges during the experience of the endeavor. The initial suspicion may be confirmed, refuted, or left open. What the author expects is that several aspects, that he did not suspect, emerged within the essays. The initial hypothesis, which he did suspect, was not the only or most important motive for the present essays. The fundamental motive was, as always, the fascination exerted by the reported experiences.

However, the initial suspicion confers a certain unity upon the essays, not only in the sense of dealing with things considered to be natural by common sense and tradition, but also in the sense that they form a discursive sequence for the following reason: in the effort to confirm or refute his suspicion, the author submitted his experiences of natural things to successive tests. He established, through these tests, several successive negations of the position of "nature." Thus, in "Rain," he sought to negate nature through "culture," in the sense of "planned manipulation." In "Cedar," through the concept of the "stranger," in the sense of nature being "natural," and that of its opposite being "introduced from outside." In "Cows," through the "artificial," in the sense of nature being spontaneous, and its opposite deliberate (technique, art). In "Grass," through the subject, in the sense of nature being an "object" of a subject that is opposed to it. In "Fingers," the author sought to see nature as a kind of "sanity" and its opposite as "oppression," "manipulation," or "apparatus." In "Moon," he sought to show nature as the late and Romantic result of culture. In "Mountains," he sought to elaborate on the opposite meanings of the concept of "history" when in relation to nature or society. In "Birds," the author made the effort to see nature as a collection of meaningful elements, and opposed it to a code that allows the reading of such a meaning. In "Valleys," he sought to see nature as a stage for humanity's drama. In "Meadows," he sought to show nature as a witness of human deeds, and therefore as a context of facts that emerge in successive levels. In "False Spring," he sought to oppose the Greek concept of nature ("*physis*") to the concept of the natural sciences. In "Wonders," he sought to do the same with the Judeo-Christian concept of nature (creation), in opposition to the concept of the natural sciences. In "Winds," he sought to elaborate the opposition between nature as "hierophany," and nature as "a transcendental commandment." In "Buds," he sought to oppose two climates that emanate from nature: that of the feeling of tragedy and that of the absurd. And in "Fog," he sought to oppose the mystification of nature by the spirit of ideology to the authentic mystery of a reality that hides as it reveals itself.

The author is perfectly aware that he did not exhaust all of the possible variants of a dialectic game that has nature as a thesis. Effectively, he came to believe that this game is practically unlimited. Whoever assumes nature as a thesis may practically assume everything else as its antithesis. In the author's opinion, this problematizes the viability of the term "nature." Such broad terms threaten to become empty and exempt of meaning. Perhaps it is time for us to abandon the term "nature" in favor of more modest and meaningful terms. This proposition, however, is obviously utopian: the term "nature" is so fundamentally rooted within our languages and thought that it will continue to hinder our concrete experience, our comprehension of this experience, and our actions.

However, there was another discovery throughout the essays that was more important than the vacuity of the term "nature." As the author applied his dialectic pairs to the contemplated phenomena, they avoided the answers. They could not be forced to answer "yes" or "no" to the two alternatives suggested. The "Rain" did not answer "yes" or "no" to the question: "is the September rain the opposite of field irrigation?" The "Fog" did not answer "yes" or "no" to the question: "is the morning fog the opposite of ideological, deliberate fog?" The phenomena gave the author unexpected answers, they confused his questions, and shattered his prejudices. The series of preceding essays obeys more or less disciplined tests, and it is in this sense that they are a discursive sequence. But as to the conclusions offered by the essays, these do not form a discursive sequence. It is as if the beginnings of the essays had been hung in a disciplined fashion onto a discursive clothesline, and as if the ends of the essays were waving disorderly in the wind that blows from stubborn and indomitable concrete experiences. Therefore, at such a level of reading, this volume presents itself as linearly discursive in relation to its intentions, and chaotically inconclusive in relation to its results. Whoever reads the essays in the order intended by the author shall verify how such a pretention was disregarded by the concrete experiences reported. The deliberately planned failed before the concreteness of things. "Naturally."

With this confession, the explanation could be taken as being satisfactory. But the author believes that he must add two asides. The first, of a more or less theoretical order, is to facilitate the insertion of this volume within the context of bookshops and libraries, and to facilitate, therefore, the labeling of this volume and its position on the appropriate shelf. The second aside, of a more subjective order, is to justify the publication of this volume within the context of today's Brazilian literature.

a) It is common to say that during the Late Middle Ages a reversal or revolution in the sensibility and valorization of the West occurred, and that consequently, a reversal or revolution in the action and passion, in the "being-in-the-world," of those who participate in such a culture also occurred. An important aspect of this reversal or revolution is the "discovery" (or "rediscovery") of nature. One of the consequences of this "discovery" is the highly curious fact that scientific knowledge initiated the progressive advance of science from the horizon toward the center. It started through the study of extremely "uninteresting" and existentially distant things (astronomy, mechanics), and advanced slowly toward more "humanly meaningful" things (biology, psychology, sociology). The history of modern science is marked by such a curious inversion of interest. It is as if scientific knowledge had deliberately suspended all the interesting subjects initially with the hope of being able to study them later, after having resolved the less interesting problems.

In the present context, the explanation of this curious phenomenon does not matter Explanations are easy, from the formal (astronomy and mechanics are mathematizable disciplines) to the historicist (the revolutionary bourgeois praxis reveals mechanisms, and its ideology conceals the social level of reality). What matters is to verify the fact that physics (the discipline that studies the movement of inanimate bodies) established itself, absurdly, as the first systematized set of modern knowledge, and in consequence, as the model for all subsequent sets. Because physics considers itself to be a "natural science," not exactly in the sense of "*physis*" (even though the term physics seems to suggest it), but because "*physis*," for the Greeks, was an animate set of animate and inanimate things, and "nature" for physics is an inanimate set of inanimate and animate things. Nevertheless, the progress of modern science is an advance from nature toward man and society.

This progress is presently coming to an end. Not only in the sense that science has extended its competence to encompass man and society, and is therefore unable to advance any further and is only able to become more detailed. In a more radical sense: science has presently come up against an insurmountable frontier. As long as scientific knowledge perambulated through extra-human regions, about which man is not existentially interested, it was possible to maintain the fiction of objective knowledge. But today, when scientific knowledge is penetrating regions in which man is implicated (interested), this fictitious distinction between the known object and the knowing subject becomes unsustainable. In these regions, man is simultaneously the object and subject of knowledge. Such a barrier, against the progress of scientific knowledge, is an important aspect of what Husserl called the crisis of Western science. In terms that are interesting within this context, that curious nature from which scientific progress started in order to invest against man and society reveals itself now as a fictionally objective horizon, and not as a solid foundation, of that concrete reality within which we are all implicated.

This crisis of the sciences (which may, in its turn, be explained as one of the reasons for a general crisis, or as the manifestation of a much deeper revolution, is not important) demands a radical reformulation of scientific methods as well as of the scientific interest for things. This reformulation is happening all around us. As for the scientific interest for things, this is currently directed at the things that are closer to us and with which we are implicated. The direction of the advance of knowledge is being inverted. As for the methods, these are founded on the interrelation between the knower and the known, and on the effects that knowledge itself has upon the knower and the known. In other words, science is becoming self-aware as the activity of a man inserted in reality that is interested in modifying it, it no longer nourishes the illusion of being the pure discipline of a man that transcends reality.

This means, among other things, that physics is no longer the model for all sciences, and those that deal with more concrete phenomena (such as communications theory) are beginning to establish themselves as models. Therefore, in a certain way, this is an "*ab ovo*" restart of the effort to scientifically understand the world that surrounds us. We are, in a certain way, just as ignorant and naive as were the first pioneers of modern science. And just as they were obliged to carry the weight of Aristotelianism on their backs, we are obliged to carry the much heavier weight of the "objective knowledge" they accumulated. It is not, certainly, a dead weight. But it is a weight that must be "put into inverted commas for future use" (to speak again of Husserl), under the pain of continuing to futilely bump up against the barrier of objectivity.

This new ignorance and naivety, to which we are condemned by our crisis, has its advantages. We may look at the world that surrounds us as if no one had ever looked at it. We are all pioneers. And as such, we may dare to do everything. For example, we may dare to endeavor to catalog the things that surround us. Since we are the first to penetrate the field, the criterion for choice in the cataloging process is ours. Those that come after may criticize us; they will be welcome to it. But at the moment, it does not matter that having an inventory is better than not having one, as long as it obeys two rules already mentioned: 1) first, the things that are interesting to us must be inventoried, and 2) we must admit that our interest for things, although imposed on us by them, turns them into things.

b) This volume, as the one published in Paris that precedes it, is an attempt at an inventory in the aforementioned sense, one of the numerous attempts currently underway. It may be labeled as "scientific," but not in the traditional meaning of the term. It is part of the context of studies ("phenomenological," "communicological," it does not matter what one calls them) that could result in a future science. That is why the results presented by the current essays are not so interesting. What is interesting is the attitude in relation to the world that is manifested through them (if such an attitude does effectively manifest itself). The author believes that, with all its failings, errors, and omissions, the present book is part of an embryonic literature which will be considered "scientific" in the future, and of which, Husserl, Ortega y Gasset, Bachelard etc. are the initiators.

This volume was written in Europe, more exactly on the outskirts of the Loire, in an alpine valley, and during trips to Europe. This fact inescapably reflects itself in the essays, and the experience with "nature" (which is their subject), is the experience of European nature. The author doubts that he would have been able to write the same type of essays within a Brazilian circumstance. Not because Brazilian nature is different from European nature, but for a deeper reason. In Europe, nature is accessible; in Brazil it is an enemy. If the author had written the essays in Brazil he would have written not about, but against nature. It would have been a different book. Not only would different aspects of nature have emerged, but also the theme itself would have been different. In Brazil the term "nature" means a different experience, value, and concept than it does in Europe. Such a difference and "overlap" of meanings is not explainable purely through geographical and historical differences between the two "worlds." It is not just the fact that Brazilian weather is "hotter" or that Brazilian society is "younger." The root of the difference is deeper, and has to do with two different existential climates. The European tends to seek shelter in nature in order to escape the threats of culture, and such a tendency is not recent (for example, it is indebted to the ideologies of Romanticism and escapism). The Greeks and the Romans were already bucolic. In Brazil, which constantly suffers from European influences, such a tendency for a "return to nature" is not unknown, but is, as so many other imported influences, little more than an empty gesture. The Brazilian, contrary to the European, has the tendency to agglomerate into densely peopled centers in order to escape the threats of nature. This manifests itself in several forms: in the "bad distribution" of the Brazilian population over the available territory; in the tendency to build high rise buildings in small cities with an excess of empty land; in the agglomeration of people on just a few of the many available beaches; in the overcrowded country clubs. Such opposed tendencies correspond to different existential climates. The European feels fundamentally threatened by the Other: it is the climate of *"homo homini lupus."* The Brazilian feels fundamentally threatened by extra-human forces. That is why the European is fundamentally engaged in the modification of society, and the Brazilian in the modification of nature. And that is why there is a fundamental (though not always palpable) solidarity within Brazilian society, which confers upon it that flavor of humanism and sympathy that is so greatly missed in Europe.

This difference, which is not an antagonism but an "overlap" (since in Brazil there are also tendencies toward an identification with nature, exemplified in Guimarães Rosa, and in Europe, strong tendencies toward an escape from nature, exemplified in the Parisian *"banlieues"*), is the source of one of the many misunderstandings between the two worlds. Europeans cannot grasp the deep Brazilian engagement against their nature, and takes such an engagement to be an alienation, since for them engagement always means a struggle in favor of a more human society. And Brazilians cannot grasp the European situation, which for them seems already completely "cultured," since for them, "to do" is to tame nature. Such a misunderstanding is tragic, because both worlds are condemned to live together, and are therefore obliged to meaningfully communicate.

Taking this fact into consideration, what emerges is the question of how to justify the publication of a volume that deals with European nature within the context of Brazilian literature. The answer to such a question would be simple had this volume been written by a European. In such a case, the justification would have been the contribution this volume could give to overcoming misunderstandings. But this is not the case: this volume was written by one who has lived the greater part of his life in Brazil, and who returned to his native Europe with a strongly Brazilianized mind and sensibilities. In other words, it was written by one who is engaged in all things Brazilian, even though, because of his biography and current geographic situation, he has a certain empathy with European nature. How then, in such a case, can the publication of this volume be justified?

The answer is curiously linked to the preceding argument that had the current epistemological crisis as its subject. One of the points raised in that paragraph was the necessity to admit the fact that the knower is implicated in the known. Therefore, the necessity to admit that "objectivity," in the sense of the knowledge of a subject that hovers above what is known, is an impossible and possibly undesirable ideal. This admission does not imply either the impossibility or the undesirability of a distancing of the knower from what is to be known. On the contrary, once "objectivity" is admitted as an impossible ideal, the distancing becomes desirable, because it can no longer be confused with an irresponsible transcendence. Such a distancing, which admits its deep involvement with what is knowable but seeks a broad and unprejudiced point of view, becomes the true post-objective scientific attitude.

An attentive reader of the present essays will verify the author's engagement in all things Brazilian between the lines that describe his experiences with European nature.

The author wrote about European nature for the Brazilian reader, not only to inform him, but also in order to dialogue with him, because the author is entirely disinterested in a possible modification of European reality. He is not inserted in it; he is a stranger and a foreigner in Europe. Such a disinterest confers a distance from the described experiences upon him. But he is interested in a possible modification of Brazilian reality through a dialogue with others. Such an interest prevents his distance from becoming an irresponsible transcendence. Because of his biographic and geographic situation, the author may serve, therefore, as a Brazilian witness to the aspects of European reality that he reported in these essays. And this is the author's justification for wanting to publish this volume in Brazil at this moment.

The reader's patience with the current explanation must be at an end at this point. There are many other things the author would have liked to add, but he must hold back his tendency to take the reader by the arm in order to seduce him to walk through the incredibly beautiful and dangerously inviting fields, meadows, woods, and mountains of Europe. He thus abandons such an attempt, and hands over, without any further ado, the present tourist guide in the hands of the Brazilian reader. "Tourist guide," as long as "tourism" is understood as an updated synonym of the term "theory." Tourism or theory is the interested, but unprejudiced view, that belongs to that provisory and estranged being in the world called "*Homo viator.*"

Univocal Publishing
123 North 3rd Street, #202
Minneapolis, MN 55401
www.univocalpublishing.com

ISBN 9781937561147
This work was composed in Berkely and Trajan.
All materials were printed and bound
in September 2013 at Univocal's atelier
in Minneapolis, USA.

The paper is Mohawk Via, Pure White Linen.
The letterpress cover was printed
on Crane's Lettra Pearl.
Both are archival quality and acid-free.

Flusser Archive Collection

Post-History

Natural: Mind

History of the Devil

Doubt

Language and Reality

Foundational Concepts of Western Thought

Philosophy of Language

The Influence of Existential Thought Today